Everyday LEADERSHIP

ATTITUDES AND ACTIONS

FOR RESPECT AND SUCCESS

MARIAM G. MacGREGOR, M.S.

Edited by Ruth Taswell

free spirit
PUBLISHING®

Copyright © 2007 by Mariam G. MacGregor, M.S.

Library of Congress Cataloging-in-Publication Data
MacGregor, Mariam G.
    Everyday leadership : attitudes and actions for respect and success, a guidebook for teens / by Mariam G. MacGregor, edited by Ruth Taswell.
        p. cm.
    ISBN-13: 978-1-57542-212-1
    ISBN-10: 1-57542-212-3
  1. Leadership. 2. Teenagers—Life skills guides. I. Taswell, Ruth. II. Title.
    HM1261.M322 2007
    646.700835—dc22

                                                    2006023186

ISBN: 978-1-57542-212-1

Free Spirit Publishing does not have control over or assume responsibility for author or third-party websites and their content. At the time of this book's publication, all facts and figures cited within are the most current available. All telephone numbers, addresses, and website URLs are accurate and active; all publications, organizations, websites, and other resources exist as described in this book; and all have been verified as of July 2021. If you find an error or believe that a resource listed here is not as described, please contact Free Spirit Publishing. Parents, teachers, and other adults: We strongly urge you to monitor children's use of the Internet.

Reading Level Grade 6; Interest Level Ages 11 & Up;
Fountas & Pinnell Guided Reading Level X

Cover and interior design by Percolator

20 19 18
Printed in the United States of America
B10950821

Free Spirit Publishing Inc.
6325 Sandburg Road, Suite 100
Minneapolis, MN 55427-3674
(612) 338-2068
help4kids@freespirit.com
freespirit.com

SUSTAINABLE FORESTRY INITIATIVE
Certified Chain of Custody
Promoting Sustainable Forestry
www.sfiprogram.org
SFI-01268

SFI label applies to the text stock

Free Spirit offers competitive pricing.
Contact edsales@freespirit.com for pricing information on multiple quantity purchases.

CONTENTS

FOREWORD

The title of this book alone, *Everyday Leadership*, highlights how every day there are opportunities for all of us to make a difference in others' lives—to provide leadership wherever we go or in whatever we do. Taking the lead isn't just for adults or a few teens who have special talents. Leadership is *everyone's* business. It's people bringing forth the best in themselves and others and acting with intention and a caring heart. It's expressing your beliefs in ways that uniquely represent you so others recognize you're the one speaking. It's seeing yourself as the answer to the question, "Why doesn't someone do something about this?"

Of course, for you to lead others, you must first believe in yourself. When working with teens, I'm constantly reminded of the power within each of us. We all have an ability to do more than what we're usually asked. This powerful book can help you discover what's within you. Written by an author who's passionate about helping *all* young people take the lead, it'll guide you in exploring who you are and what you care about. You'll gain more confidence in yourself and uncover an ability to do more than you may ever have thought possible.

Barry Z. Posner, Ph.D.
Coauthor, *The Leadership Challenge* and *A Leader's Legacy*

A Leadership Attitude

Have you ever wished you felt more confident? Had more respect from your friends and classmates? Or that adults and others really heard what you had to say?

As a teen, you have many exciting paths to explore. You may feel overwhelmed by the possibilities or pressure to please a lot of people. When it seems unclear which path to take, it's human nature to wonder, "Who *am* I?" "What *do* I care about?" "How *can* I make a difference?"

Let this book inspire you to discover some of the answers to these questions, as you look at what it means to take the lead in everyday situations and in out-of-the-ordinary ones.

We all know about the importance of having a positive attitude, but what about a "leadership attitude"? Just as anyone can choose to have a positive attitude, anyone can learn to have a leadership attitude. With a leadership attitude, you take action while others may sit on the side. You learn about yourself while learning to lead.

The activities you'll participate in and write about using this book are activities that have helped other teens develop a leadership attitude. As a result, these teens said that they:

- Felt more confident speaking in front of others and figuring out conflicts

- Got better grades

- Did more extracurricular activities

- Liked having others see them as part of the solution, not part of the problem

- Cared more about doing positive things in their community

- Showed more interest in education after high school (for example, voluntarily took college entrance exams, went to college information sessions, or applied for financial aid before graduating from high school)

You don't need to be someone "special" to take the lead. Leadership isn't just for adults, politicians, authority figures, or the rich and famous. Still, finding personally meaningful ways to take the lead can be challenging. Perhaps you shy away from leadership because you're afraid of making a mistake or of "failing" in front of others. Maybe you think you don't have what it takes or have been told you're too young. Maybe others perceive you as a troublemaker and you don't believe they'll see you as a leader. Or possibly, you *do* find yourself drawn to being a leader and are trying to identify ways to act on your abilities.

Many times leadership opportunities, big and small, are right in front of you. Sometimes they are things you already are doing. With a leadership attitude, you recognize when you take the lead or when you can. Being a leader motivates you to try new things and find out more about what you believe in. Being a leader inspires you to discover how to successfully make a difference in the world around you—how to reach your own potential as a unique person.

HOW TO USE THIS GUIDE

This guide is divided into 21 sessions about different topics on leadership. The sessions are meetings you and other teens in your group or class will participate in with your group leader or teacher.

The quotes at the beginning of each session are triggers to jumpstart your thoughts about the leadership skills you're learning. Reflecting on what the quotes are saying or make you think about allows you to consider how closely they capture your own feelings about leadership. If possible, share your thoughts with others.

For each session, you'll also find two sections titled "Think and Write About It" and "Do Something About It." Some sessions may also have other sections titled "Try This" and "Find Out More About It." "Try This" pages coordinate with an activity you may do during a session, or which you could also do later if you miss a session. "Find Out More About It" pages provide background information or additional reading on the session topic, and also are good reference materials for other times in your life when you encounter a situation or want to know a little more as you practice your leadership skills.

For the "Think and Write About It" pages, your group leader or teacher will ask you to write responses to a few or all of the questions. The questions relate to the session activity. They also help you connect what you are learning with how leadership relates to everyday life.

This book is a place to write honestly and sincerely about your ideas on leadership. After completing group activities and discussions in a session, you may be thinking, "Yeah, I get it," so it may seem unnecessary to reflect and write about your experiences. But reflecting is important! Expressing your thoughts in writing gives you a way to commit to what you just "got" from the leadership session. When you have an idea in your head, it's easy to just mull it over day after day. But when you put that thought onto paper, you take another step toward actually doing something. Use a notebook or folder to store pictures, session handouts, notes, mementos, or other things from your experiences as a leader that you want to remember.

To help build your confidence about sharing, write—or discuss during sessions—only what you're comfortable knowing others may read or ask you about. Interacting with others in your group helps you gain insight into yourself. And sharing your writing and ideas promotes the everyday connections you're making about leadership. It also helps you understand what other people are learning or going through and guides you to become the type of leader you would want to work with on a team.

Although you and your friends may discover similar expectations about leaders, each person has his or her own leadership style. Even though everyone in your group is learning the same leadership skills, you'll probably interpret them differently. Being an effective leader is knowing how to work as part of a team, appreciating others for their contributions, and learning how to take appropriate risks. Being an effective leader also is about recognizing when you don't have all the answers and knowing how to still carry on. So talk about the skills, practice them together, and look for ways you can learn more about leadership and inspire others around you.

At the end of each session, you will be asked to select a goal or two from the "Do Something About It" pages to put your leadership attitude, knowledge, and skills into action. The goals echo themes of the session activities. These acts can be simple to undertake or require greater personal stretching to accomplish. You may get nervous taking the first steps, but remember those steps don't always have to be hard. No matter what, the greatest step is committing to take action. The more actions you choose, the more you learn. Each "Do Something About It" page includes blank lines for you to add your own, maybe more personal, ideas.

Put a check next to the goals you select that will demonstrate your leadership abilities and write the specific date by which you will complete them; then record when you actually reach a goal and describe what you did. Although you may achieve some goals quickly, others take time, preparation, and teamwork. Some goals are ongoing and, even if you set a date by which to "complete" them, they can soon become new habits or regular behaviors (for example, daily, once a week, twice a month).

You may already know what it's like to set goals such as those in the "Do Something About It" pages, or this may be a first. Either way, challenge yourself to select actions that are reasonable and help you take being a leader to the next level.

To open yourself up to what the world has to offer and make a difference, developing a leadership attitude and committing to taking action are essential. What choices can you make today that will expand your personal leadership attitude? What other opportunities can you find to expand your commitment as a leader and change maker? Let this book and what you learn in all your leadership experiences guide you to discover what's truly possible within and because of you. If you have a leadership experience you'd like to share, write to me in care of Free Spirit Publishing Inc., 6325 Sandburg Road, Suite 100, Minneapolis, MN 55427, or at help4kids@freespirit.com.

In closing, a note of thanks to all my past students, especially the ones who never believed they had the "right stuff" to be leaders, and who often proved everyone, including themselves, wrong.

Thanks also to the teens on my virtual advisory board, who provide insight and honest feedback about issues important to teen leaders and whether the things I write are actually interesting to teens. If you would like to become part of my virtual board in the future, email me at mariam@youthleadership.com.

Mariam G. MacGregor, M.S.

INTRODUCING LEADERSHIP

> Each one of you has something no one else has, or has ever had: your fingerprints, your brain, your heart. Be an individual. Be unique. Stand out. Make noise. Make someone notice. That's the power of individuals.
>
> —**Jon Bon Jovi,** musician and singer

> A great tennis career is something that a 15-year-old normally doesn't have. I hope my example helps other teens believe they can accomplish things they never thought possible!
>
> —**Maria Sharapova,** world-class professional Russian tennis player

When you find yourself facing a situation or problem you wish you could change, what do you do? When you discover something new or exciting you'd like to achieve, do you act on your ideas or hesitate? What makes you unsure? Sometimes, people hold back on trying to fulfill their hopes or dreams because they want to fit in with peers or please friends. Sometimes, they don't act because they're scared to try. But often, they simply don't know what steps to take. Committing to learning how to take the lead can help you figure out what the most effective steps are. The question then becomes: What *will* you do?

Think and Write About It

In this session's activity, you imagined yourself some years from now as an accomplished leader on the cover of a fictitious magazine. Now think about ways you already are a leader. Consider what you do every day and what you care about: how you help your family, groups at school or where you live, a part-time job, your attitudes. Reflect on ways you have changed because of your involvement. If you aren't sure of your own leadership skills, think about what you want to do. Write your responses to one or more of the following statements or questions.

I consider myself a leader at _____ because

_____

_____

I don't consider myself a leader at _____ because

_____

_____

People at _____ consider me to be a leader because

_____

_____

People at _____ don't consider me to be a leader because

_____

_____

_____

When you think of yourself as a leader, what expectations do you have of yourself?

_____

_____

_____

What expectations do you feel others have of you as a leader?

_____

_____

_____

Do Something About It

To commit to learning about leadership, it's important to put your thoughts into action. Choosing to act can help you take being a leader to the next level, assist you in finding out more about yourself, or inspire you to do something that before now you couldn't imagine doing.

Check the goal(s) you will set to demonstrate your leadership abilities. If you have ideas of your own that you prefer, add them on the lines provided. Then write a date by which you plan to put your goal(s) into action on the "To Do By" lines and the date you completed them on the "Did By" lines. Be sure to fill in "What I Did to Achieve My Goal(s)."

	To Do By	Did By
○ I will do what I can to help a new teen in my neighborhood, school, or youth group feel welcome.	_____	_____
○ I will sit next to someone other than one of my friends in one of my classes or other activities and offer my help.	_____	

	To Do By	Did By

○ I will find out what teen leadership positions are available at school or with a community group or program.

○ I will talk with my friends or family about the ways they think I am already a leader.

Other "Do Something About It" Ideas

○ _____

_____

_____

○ _____

_____

_____

What I Did to Achieve My Goal(s)

_____

_____

_____

_____

_____

_____

_____

WHAT LEADERSHIP MEANS TO ME

> I suppose leadership at one time meant muscles;
> but today it means getting along with people.
>
> **—Indira Gandhi,** two-term prime minister, India

> Leadership is action, not position.
>
> **—Donald H. McGannon,** former president of Westinghouse
> Broadcasting Co. and the National Urban League

When you hear the word *leadership,* what or who comes to mind? People describe leadership in so many ways that even experts can't agree on a single meaning. Aside from the standard dictionary explanation, many definitions refer to the position of leadership that someone holds—often with a title that shows the person has control over others. People often think leadership is about a leader getting others to do what he or she wants. But getting people to do something is just one aspect of being a leader. In fact, leadership—and leaders—comes in all shapes and sizes with all kinds of attitudes and abilities.

TRY THIS

Defining Leadership

With at least two other people, brainstorm any words, positive and negative, that come to mind when you think of *leadership*. Remember, when you brainstorm with others, *all* ideas are accepted. Write every characteristic your group comes up with below. Then put a plus sign (+) next to the words that could be positive and a minus sign (–) next to those that could be negative. Mark both plus and minus signs next to words you consider both positive and negative. Be sure to list words, not names of people.

_____   _____   _____

_____   _____   _____

_____   _____   _____

_____   _____   _____

_____   _____   _____

_____   _____   _____

Think and Write About It

It can be really satisfying when you're able to take the lead and meet your and other people's expectations of a leader. One way to accomplish this is to understand what leadership means to the people you're leading.

You can begin by exploring different definitions of leadership. One definition to highlight comes from Warren G. Bennis, Ph.D., who many people consider to be the "leadership guru" because of his numerous contributions worldwide to the field of leadership. He defines *leadership* as:

> "knowing yourself, having a vision that is well communicated, building trust among colleagues, and taking effective action to realize your own leadership potential."*

---

* Bennis, Warren G., *On Becoming a Leader* (New York: Perseus Publishing, 2003).

More simply, leadership is being clear about who you are and what you care about, and doing what needs to be done. Consider this definition, and any others you know, as you write your responses to the questions and statements that follow.

Review the characteristics of leadership from your list on page 10 (or the larger group's list). Select the ones that mean the most to you and explain why each one is important to you.

_____

_____

_____

_____

When people refer to you as a leader, what do you hope they are saying or thinking about you?

_____

_____

_____

_____

I want others to consider me a leader because:

_____

_____

_____

_____

People who are considered leaders should be expected to:

_____

_____

_____

_____

I define *leadership* as:

_____

_____

_____

_____

Do Something About It

Think about your own definition of leadership and the characteristics you associate with it. What steps will you take to demonstrate or build these traits in yourself?

Check the goal(s) you will set to demonstrate your leadership abilities. If you have ideas of your own that you prefer, add them on the lines provided. Then write a date by which you plan to put your goal(s) into action on the "To Do By" lines and the date you completed them on the "Did By" lines. Be sure to fill in "What I Did to Achieve My Goal(s)."

	To Do By	Did By
○ I will ask someone I respect to tell me about a more experienced and admired person he or she got advice from and how that person affected him or her.	_____	_____
○ I will pick a subject I'm good at and ask a teacher if I can tutor younger students or peers for 8 to 10 sessions.	_____	_____

	To Do By	Did By
○ I will interview a community leader and ask for his or her definition of leadership. I will share what I learn with this group.	_____	_____
○ I will cowrite with a friend an article for the school or local newspaper, or a community program newsletter about the leadership abilities of teens.	_____	_____

Other "Do Something About It" Ideas

○ _____   _____   _____

_____

_____

○ _____   _____   _____

_____

_____

What I Did to Achieve My Goal(s)

_____

_____

_____

_____

_____

_____

_____

SESSION · SESSION · SESSION · SESSION · SESSION · SESSION

THE LEADERS IN MY LIFE

> The most dangerous leadership myth is that leaders are born—that there is a genetic factor to leadership. This myth asserts that people simply either have certain charismatic qualities or not. That's nonsense; in fact, the opposite is true. Leaders are made rather than born.
>
> **—Warren G. Bennis, Ph.D.,** author of more than 25 books on leadership and founder of the University of Southern California Leadership Institute

> It's far more impressive when others discover your good qualities without your help.
>
> **—Judith Martin,** novelist and journalist better known as Miss Manners

Everyone can be a leader. That may seem hard to believe, especially if you feel being a leader doesn't come easily for you. But every person has a combination of different personal characteristics, or qualities of leadership, that can make it possible to take the lead—or learn how. Some people think all it takes is a single characteristic, like self-confidence, to be a leader, but one characteristic doesn't make you a leader. Successful leaders use different combinations of leadership qualities in various ways, leading by words, by attitude, and by action.

TRY THIS

Qualities of Leadership

Identifying well-known people who demonstrate effective leadership
qualities helps you relate to how others interpret those qualities. Read
each of the following qualities and fill in the blanks with the name of a well-known
person who shows that quality. It's not unusual for well-known leaders to have
more than one quality, but try to name a different person for each quality. If you
get stuck, think about people locally or nationally you've read about in newspapers
or magazines, or heard about on radio or TV recently.

A Well-Known Leader Who
DOES THE RIGHT THING: _____

Leaders who do the right thing know how they feel about issues and take the high
road, even in difficult situations and when others aren't watching. They are ethical,
act with integrity, have good morals, and know how to stand up for their beliefs.

A Well-Known Leader Who
HAS A SENSE OF DIRECTION: _____

Leaders with a sense of direction have a "built-in GPS system." They know how
to move from Point A to Point B, even when things get in the way. Their vision
extends beyond the present day and beyond themselves; they recognize that setting
goals and being purposeful keeps them and others motivated on the journey.

A Well-Known Leader Who
RESPECTS POWER: _____

Leaders who respect power recognize their responsibility in using their power. They
do not use their power carelessly or irresponsibly or to take advantage of situations.

A Well-Known Leader Who
THINKS CREATIVELY: _____

Leaders who think creatively know how to look at opportunities and problems in
new ways or differently from others around them. They see the possibility that
exists and ask, "Why not?"

A Well-Known Leader Who
EMBRACES DIFFERENCES: _____

Leaders who embrace differences recognize how diverse our world is. They recognize that people with different beliefs, backgrounds, and expectations often need to work together. They strive to promote understanding from all sides and bring dissimilar groups together to explore new directions.

A Well-Known Leader Who
ACTS WITH PASSION: _____

Leaders who act with passion inspire others. They communicate their excitement about a task in both subtle and obvious ways.

A Well-Known Leader Who
MANAGES UNEXPECTED SITUATIONS: _____

Leaders who manage unexpected situations know that success requires more than good planning. They think before acting and try to consider the outcome of options, even when time is limited.

A Well-Known Leader Who
MODELS HUMILITY: _____

Leaders who model humility (or modesty) act to make a difference. They don't call attention to their accomplishments and talent. They don't brag, seek praise for achievements, or have any hidden motives.

Think and Write About It

Leadership happens all the time; every person has the potential to be a leader. For each of the following leadership qualities, write the name of someone you know *personally* who demonstrates it. Choose a different individual for each quality, even though one person in your life may possess more than one of these qualities. Describe in what ways each person demonstrates the quality.

A Person I Know Well Who
DOES THE RIGHT THING: _____

_____

_____

A Person I Know Well Who
HAS A SENSE OF DIRECTION: _____

_____

_____

A Person I Know Well Who
RESPECTS POWER: _____

_____

_____

A Person I Know Well Who
THINKS CREATIVELY: _____

_____

_____

A Person I Know Well Who
EMBRACES DIFFERENCES: _____

_____

_____

A Person I Know Well Who
ACTS WITH PASSION: _____

_____

A Person I Know Well Who
MANAGES UNEXPECTED SITUATIONS: _____

_____

_____

A Person I Know Well Who
MODELS HUMILITY: _____

_____

_____

Do Something About It

Think of people who are leaders in your life and the qualities they demonstrate. Now consider the qualities you show others in accomplishing what you set out to do.

Check the goal(s) you will set to demonstrate your leadership abilities. If you have ideas of your own that you prefer, add them on the lines provided. Then write a date by which you plan to put your goal(s) into action on the "To Do By" lines and the date you completed them on the "Did By" lines. Be sure to fill in "What I Did to Achieve My Goal(s)."

	To Do By	Did By
○ I will write a thank-you letter to someone who has been a leader to me.	_____	_____
○ I will nominate a friend, mentor, or family member for a community award (sponsored by a local TV station, newspaper, organization, government office, or other agency) that recognizes valuable contributions to our community.	_____	_____

	To Do By	Did By
○ I will interview an elder to get a different generation's perspective on leadership qualities as well as to get advice for young leaders. I will share what I learn with this group.	_____	_____
○ I will write about three other leadership qualities (not included on the "Qualities of Leadership" list on pages 15–16) that are important to me and explain why I value these traits.	_____	_____

Other "Do Something About It" Ideas

○ _____   _____   _____

_____

_____

○ _____   _____   _____

_____

_____

What I Did to Achieve My Goal(s)

_____

_____

_____

_____

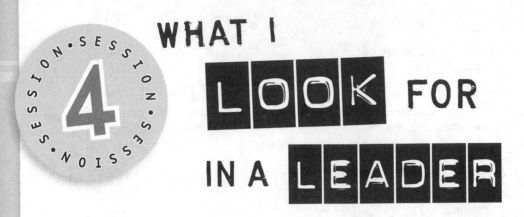

SESSION 4

WHAT I LOOK FOR IN A LEADER

> In Iroquois society, leaders are encouraged to remember seven generations in the past and consider seven generations in the future when making decisions that affect the people.
>
> **—Wilma P. Mankiller,** former principal chief, Cherokee Nation of Oklahoma

> Treat a man as he is, and he will remain as he is. Treat a man as he could be, and he will become what he should be.
>
> **—Ralph Waldo Emerson,** American poet and essayist

Taking the lead can be a tough balancing act. What's important to you as a leader may differ from what's important to someone else. Getting everyone in a group to agree on priorities often can be even tougher. What people expect from or look for in a leader—either individually or as a group—has a huge impact on what they're willing to do. As you develop your leadership qualities, keep in mind everyone's expectations to help make things happen.

An Effective Leader

Read the following statements. Which five actions would you rank as most important for a leader directing a group project, such as a food drive or class presentation? Place a number from 1 (most important) to 5 (least important) to the left of the corresponding statement. Prior to ranking, add other leadership behaviors you believe are significant to the blank lines that follow the statements.

_____ The leader gives background information and explains why it's important to do the project.

_____ The leader specifically explains each person's role in the project.

_____ The leader asks for and listens to everyone's suggestions.

_____ The leader gives group members a choice of tasks to perform on the project.

_____ The leader is very enthusiastic about the project.

_____ The leader treats everyone as equals and works toward creating an atmosphere where using her or his authority is rarely needed.

_____ The leader keeps group members informed about what is going on and communicates the reasons for making important decisions.

_____ The leader listens kindly to complaints or concerns.

_____ The leader never criticizes or puts down someone in front of others.

_____ The leader values the differences each person brings to the group.

_____ The leader is sympathetic if someone makes a mistake and doesn't make it a big issue.

_____ The leader openly and freely praises excellent work.

_____ The leader encourages challenging the status quo and seeks ways to improve teamwork.

_____ The leader regularly meets with members to discuss ways to improve the group's success.

_____ The leader keeps cool under pressure and controls her or his temper.

● ●

Other important leadership behaviors:

___ _____

___ _____

___ _____

TRY THIS

An Effective Leader: The Group's View

Read the Effective Leader statements again. Work with the rest of your class or group to rank *together* the top five actions needed for a leader directing a group project, such as a food drive or class presentation. Place a number from 1 (most important) to 5 (least important) to the left of your original rankings. Prior to ranking, add other expectations the group believes are significant to the blank lines that follow the statements. Your group must agree on the final ranking, even if individually you prefer to rank them differently. If you have time, consider identifying (not necessarily ranking) the next top five actions and the five actions the group feels are least important.

Think and Write About It

Prioritizing what *you* want from a leader versus what the *group* wants requires different mindsets. When you're working with a group to agree on some goals (as in the session activity), each person in the group may experience interesting reactions or emotions. Keep your own reactions in mind as you answer the following questions and statements. Use the lines provided to write your responses.

What is it like to have to compromise or negotiate on your priorities for the benefit of your group?

_____

_____

_____

What do you think it takes for a group to make a decision together?

_____

_____

_____

What role do you think the leader should play when a group needs to make a decision?

_____

_____

_____

I often find myself thinking/doing _____ when I'm part of a group making a decision. During the next group activity I participate in, either with this group or in a different setting, I will try to:

_____

_____

_____

Do Something About It

Try selecting actions from the following goals that inspire you to act in different ways than you're used to in groups. The skills you'll build in various situations will help as you participate in other groups. And whether or not you're the leader, you can help balance everyone's priorities, including your own.

Check the goal(s) you will set to demonstrate your leadership abilities. If you have ideas of your own that you prefer, add them on the lines provided. Then write a date by which you plan to put your goal(s) into action on the "To Do By" lines and the date you completed them on the "Did By" lines. Be sure to fill in "What I Did to Achieve My Goal(s)."

	To Do By	Did By

○ I will help a friend or classmate on a project not because it necessarily interests me, but because he or she wants my help.

○ I will discuss a controversial topic with someone who holds an opposing view without trying to convince him or her of my opinion.

○ I will join a group or committee that needs more volunteers even though I tend to be nervous with new groups at first.

○ I will tell my friends when I really need to be by myself, even though they may be disappointed or get mad at me for not doing something with the group.

Other "Do Something About It" Ideas

○ _____

_____

_____

What I Did to Achieve My Goal(s)

_____

_____

_____

_____

_____

LEADERS AND FOLLOWERS

> If your actions inspire others to dream more, learn more,
> do more and become more, you are a leader.
>
> **—John Quincy Adams,** 6th U.S. President

> Leadership is a two-way street, loyalty
> up and loyalty down. Respect for one's superiors
> and care for one's crew.
>
> **—Grace Murray Hopper,** Rear Admiral and pioneer computer scientist

Everyone works better with a leader whose way of leading just fits. Depending on who's in your group, your usual leadership style may not succeed as well as you'd like. Before you choose to lead a group in a particular way, it helps to understand what everyone in the group needs in order to do their best. Some people prefer very specific directions; others favor fewer guidelines. If necessary, adjust your leadership style to be the leader your group needs you to be.

Douglas McGregor's* Human Behavior Theories

Theory Y: Leaders believe the people in their group ("Y" people) are very capable and self-motivated, requiring little direction.

Theory X: Leaders believe the people in their group ("X" people) are not as capable and self-motivated and prefer to be told what to do.

Leaders themselves are neither Y nor X people; rather, they are "group-centered" or "leader-centered" in how they lead the people in their group.

Y and X behavior can change depending on the project that needs to be done and the individual makeup of the group and the leader.

Neither group-centered nor leader-centered leadership is necessarily the best way to lead a group. What's important for an effective leader to recognize is his or her own behavior and how he or she views the individuals in the group.

For example, when group members are excited and motivated by what they are doing, they won't necessarily need a lot of direction or structure (they're Y people with a group-centered leader). With a different set of circumstances, however, these same people may be more productive if told what to do and how to do it (they're X people with a leader-centered leader).

Now ask yourself:

- How do you generally see yourself as a leader? How about as a follower?

- How do you tend to see the people in your group when you're the leader?

- What type of leader most motivates you when you're a member of a group?

To learn more about leaders and followers working together, see session 13 about team building.

---

*McGregor, Douglas, *The Human Side of Enterprise*, annotated ed. (New York: McGraw-Hill, 2006).

Think and Write About It

While some leaders are group-centered and some leader-centered, most people in leadership roles generally use a combination of approaches to lead a group, depending on the situation. For example, if you are captain of a sports team that has been together for some time, you'll likely use more of a group-centered leadership style. You realize the group doesn't need much direction from you. If you're a camp leader training a new group of counselors, you're more likely to be directive and leader-centered to make sure the counselors are prepared to work with young kids. You recognize there's a lot of information they must learn, with little room for mistakes.

As you respond to the following questions and statements, keep in mind different situations you've experienced with the same leader. Consider whether the leader used different approaches in guiding the group, depending on who was in the group at the time.

Write about a leadership experience of your own or one you observed where you felt a group-centered leadership style was effective. Describe the situation, how people were treated in the group (as Ys or Xs), and why the style was effective.

_____

_____

_____

_____

Write about a leadership experience of your own or one you observed where you felt that a leader-centered leadership style was effective. Describe the situation, how people were treated in the group (as Ys or Xs), and why the style was effective.

_____

_____

_____

_____

When you take the lead with groups, either in a formal role or under more everyday circumstances, do you tend to use a group-centered or a leader-centered leadership approach? Write your answer and explain why this approach is a natural fit for you or if it's a style you would like to change.

_____

_____

_____

Based on what you learned about McGregor's Theory Y and Theory X (see page 26), write what you've discovered about how you treat people in groups (as Ys or Xs).

_____

_____

_____

Do Something About It

Gaining awareness of how you treat others in a group as well as how you like to be treated in a group can help you fine-tune your leadership style. Doing this takes time and practice. You may discover that in one situation you act one way, and in another situation you act differently—this is human nature.

Check the goal(s) you will set to demonstrate your leadership abilities. If you have ideas of your own that you prefer, add them on the lines provided. Then write a date by which you plan to put your goal(s) into action on the "To Do By" lines and the date you completed them on the "Did By" lines. Be sure to fill in "What I Did to Achieve My Goal(s)."

	To Do By	Did By
○ I will offer to show a substitute teacher or new staff member around and help deal with new or difficult situations during a class or an activity.	_____	_____

	To Do By	Did By
○ I will be the first to volunteer in a situation that requires a group leader.		
○ I will try to recruit someone new to help with a club or an organization project.		
○ I will take time to listen to others' ideas and resist insisting that I know how to deal with a situation.		

Other "Do Something About It" Ideas

○ _____

_____

_____

○ _____

_____

_____

What I Did to Achieve My Goal(s)

_____

_____

_____

_____

_____

_____

_____

SESSION · SESSION · SESSION · SESSION · SESSION

6

POWER PLAY

> The most common way people give up their power is by thinking they don't have any.
>
> **—Alice Walker,** American author

> The measure of a man is what he does with power.
>
> **—Plato,** ancient Greek philosopher

Power impacts many relationships in everyday life—how a parent or guardian may treat you, how a teacher or coach directs you, how politicians get laws passed, and more. Leaders are able to accomplish certain goals based upon the power they have with people who follow their lead. In some cases, informal leaders—those who are not officially in a leadership position of a group—may have just as much (or sometimes more) power than the official leader.

Just as leadership is identified in many ways, so is power. And just as a leader may emphasize different leadership qualities depending on the situation, a leader may also use different types of power.

What You Know or Who You Know?

Leaders are able to accomplish certain goals based upon the power they have with their group, and how they got it or use it. Here are seven types of power. Each one includes an example of how a leader can use that power and possible positive or negative results. An effective leader seeks to use different types of power positively, rather than one particular style exclusively.

REWARD POWER is based on a leader's ability to give rewards and positive consequences if people do what is asked of them.

Example: While shopping at the grocery store, a father promises his daughter a candy bar if she will be quiet until they are done.

- *Positive effect:* The potential for a reward motivates the daughter to be quiet.

- *Negative effect:* Once the daughter realizes her father's strategy, she may only be quiet if she gets candy. She also won't learn the basic value of proper behavior.

REFERENT POWER is based on a leader's likeability. People often are willing to do as the leader asks because they like or want to be like this person.

Example: An admired friend encourages you to do well academically.

- *Positive effect:* A person's admiration for someone who offers encouragement inspires the person to do well.

- *Negative effect:* Admiration for another person and "encouragement" from that person in the form of peer pressure can also inspire making poor choices, such as cheating in order to get a better grade.

LEGITIMATE POWER is based on a leader's position. People see the position as one that gives the leader power.

Example: Political figures, government officers, police, teachers, principals, student council members, youth group leaders, or athletic team captains are all leaders whose positions represent legitimate power.

- *Positive effect:* While someone holds a certain position, people respect and respond to him or her in that position.

- *Negative effect:* Just because an individual holds a leadership position doesn't mean the person is an effective or admirable leader.

INFORMATION POWER is based on a leader's control of or access to information that is perceived as valuable.

Example: The adult advisor to a youth group knows what other adult decision makers in the organization would support or disapprove of regarding possible youth activities.

- *Positive effect:* This person can share information with the youth group to help propose some activities rather than have the group spend a lot of time strategizing for something that is not likely to get approved.

- *Negative effect:* This person could inappropriately share other decision makers' preferences with the youth group. Or this person could prevent sharing information from the youth group with the other decision makers.

EXPERT POWER is based on a leader's expertise, skill, and knowledge. People respect the leader's expertise and are influenced by it.

Example: Doctors, scientists, lawyers, professors, athletes, or anyone who has a great deal of experience in a particular field, activity, or hobby.

- *Positive effect:* People can get the best and most accurate information from people who are considered experts.

- *Negative effect:* An expert could take advantage of someone by providing incomplete or misleading information. This may influence a person to make a decision that he or she might not make otherwise with the right information.

CONNECTION POWER is based on who a leader knows. People see the leader as having power because of his or her connections to or relationships with influential or important people.

Example: A high school senior knows a parent who is an alumnus of a nearby private college. The alumnus can get the student an interview with the Admissions Office.

- *Positive effect:* Connections can help people obtain important things, such as a recommendation, a job, acceptance into a school or special program, tickets to a show, or passes backstage to meet a performer.

- *Negative effect:* Connections can mean some people get certain things without deserving them, or keep others from getting what they deserve.

COERCIVE POWER is based on a leader's ability to invoke fear in people. The leader has the ability to take away privileges or punish those who do not cooperate.

Example: A parent who insists you complete a project exactly the way he or she says or else you can't do something you were hoping to do.

- *Positive effect:* Sometimes, setting specific rules is the only way to get a job done.

- *Negative effect:* Often, threatening punishment doesn't help people recognize the value of the project.

FIND OUT MORE ABOUT IT

Making Things Happen

To get things done and use their power, leaders apply different styles. Some draw on their *authority,* the process of insisting or demanding that others do a task; others use *influence,* a way of persuading that's less direct or obvious. Both styles are ways of expressing power, and leaders can use them with positive and negative effects.

Think and Write About It

Certain types of power are used in different settings. For example, legitimate power relates most obviously to governmental leaders. For each type of power listed (see "What You Know or Who You Know?" on pages 31–33 for definitions), write about situations where you saw this power in action—a time when it was used positively, and another when it was used negatively. If possible, write about situations where you were the one using the type of power. Be specific.

REWARD POWER

Positive use: _____

Negative use: _____

REFERENT POWER

Positive use: _____

Negative use: _____

LEGITIMATE POWER

Positive use: _____

Negative use: _____

INFORMATION POWER

Positive use: _____

Negative use: _____

EXPERT POWER

Positive use: _____

Negative use: _____

CONNECTION POWER

Positive use: _____

Negative use: _____

COERCIVE POWER

Positive use: _____

Negative use: _____

Do Something About It

To increase others' awareness of you as a leader, try expressing your personal power in different ways to see what works well when. For example, if you tend to use authority to get things done, try using influence. If you mostly use influence, try authority.

Check the goal(s) you will set to demonstrate your leadership abilities. If you have ideas of your own that you prefer, add them on the lines provided. Then write a date by which you plan to put your goal(s) into action on the "To Do By" lines and the date you completed them on the "Did By" lines. Be sure to fill in "What I Did to Achieve My Goal(s)."

	To Do By	Did By
○ I will survey others at school or in my community group to see if they will help me resolve an issue we've been complaining about.	_____	_____
○ I will ask a friend to help me interview a teacher, coach, parent, trusted adult, or business or religious leader about his or her views on using power. I will write about what we learn and if possible share it with the group.	_____	_____
○ I will contribute to the decision-making process with my friends as we plan to do something together. If I normally dominate decisions made with my friends, I will listen to or ask for their opinions. I will not push everyone just to do what I want. If I'm normally quiet and just agree to what others suggest, I'll voice my opinion.	_____	_____
○ I will register to vote, if that is an option for me, and let others know why I think it is important to vote.	_____	_____

Other "Do Something About It" Ideas   To Do By   Did By

○ _____   _____   _____

  _____

  _____

  _____

○ _____   _____   _____

  _____

  _____

  _____

What I Did to Achieve My Goal(s)

_____

_____

_____

_____

_____

_____

_____

_____

_____

COMMUNICATE WITH STYLE

> *A boo is a lot louder than a cheer. If you have 10 people cheering and one person booing, all you hear is the booing.*
>
> **—Lance Armstrong,** American cyclist, seven-time winner of the Tour de France

> *Ninety percent of leadership is the ability to communicate something people want.*
>
> **—Dianne Feinstein,** U.S. Senator, California

What you say and how you say it has a major impact on your success as a leader. Noticing how others communicate also is important. When you're speaking, what's the first thing you observe about listeners? Can you "read between the lines" when someone shares information with you? Whether your goal is making a positive first impression or building a relationship, uncovering your communication strengths will affect how well you get your message across to others.

37

What You <u>Don't</u> Say Can Say It All

Nonverbal responses—what our bodies, eyes, and faces express when we are talking or listening to others—are important to communicating successfully.

Posture

How and where you stand can have meaning. Standing above someone who is sitting often indicates control over that person. Leaning forward generally implies interest in the person or topic of discussion, slouching implies boredom or disinterest. Crossing your arms over your chest may mean you believe you are better than the other person.

Voice

Your tone of voice (loud or soft, clear or mumbled, with what emotion) can significantly change what you say.

Gestures

Ideally, gestures match your verbal messages, although they can make whoever's listening react in certain ways.

Eye Contact

Eye contact can help show and maintain attention and interest.

Facial Expressions

Facial expressions are both the easiest *and* most difficult nonverbal cues to control. They can send a message before you even say anything.

Appearance

The clothes you wear and how you style your hair are expressions of your individuality. But when making a presentation or representing a school or community group, it's important to consider your audience and show respect for a group. To help your message get heard, make choices regarding your appearance appropriate for your audience.

For more about communication skills, see "Find Out More About It" in sessions 8 and 19.

How You Say It

Giving or getting constructive feedback often helps people make decisions and take action. The following guidelines offer tips for *giving* helpful feedback; they also provide guidance on what to look for when asking others to give you feedback.

- Focus on a particular statement or behavior, rather than on the person, who may feel a need to defend himself or herself.

- Provide information that is valuable, not because it feels good to say what you're really thinking.

- Seek clarification on *what* was said, instead of reacting to *why* you think the person said what she or he said. By offering descriptions rather than judgments, you can avoid making assumptions about another person's intent or motivation.

- Create an opportunity to share and suggest ideas, rather than tell someone specifically what to do. Seek possible choices rather than just look for a single solution.

- Avoid overloading a person with too much information at once. Suggest you talk about other points at another time.

- Focus on the current situation or conversation rather than past circumstances.

- Choose an appropriate time to give (or request) feedback. If a person is busy or distracted, he or she may easily misconstrue well-intended positive feedback.

For more about communication skills, see "Find Out More About It" in sessions 8 and 19.

Think and Write About It

To give and receive feedback successfully, consider how you communicate with others whether speaking, listening, or sending nonverbal messages. For each of the following statements, rate yourself on a scale from 1 to 5, with 1 indicating you do it well and 5 meaning you need to improve in this area. Write the number on the blank line next to each statement. Think of a variety of circumstances for each statement to determine a realistic rating.

It's easier to boost your leadership talents and to communicate with style when you're more aware of your communication skills. Keep in mind the statements you rated as lower and try to improve them. You can practice them in everyday conversations, when you take on leadership roles, an in upcoming sessions.

_____ I can influence or help others when I communicate as well as be open to others' comments when they communicate with me.

_____ I stay aware of my prejudices and values so I am able to listen, empathize, and understand others' viewpoints as well as avoid misspeaking.

_____ I accept that it is my responsibility to clarify what I am saying if others don't understand me.

_____ I listen because I know I'm learning little if I keep talking and don't let anyone else say anything.

_____ I make sure I understand what others are saying.

_____ I pay attention to nonverbal messages and try to notice the feelings or motives behind people's words, even though I can't know exactly what someone else is thinking or feeling.

_____ I am an attentive listener and let the person speaking know I'm listening by nodding, using direct eye contact, or other nonverbal gestures.

_____ I make a special attempt to listen carefully when I disagree with what someone else is saying.

_____ I realize being a good listener doesn't mean I must agree with what another person is saying.

_____ I try to stay calm and not overreact to emotionally charged words or comments.

_____ I consider who's giving the feedback, how she or he is saying it, and the situation in which it's being told. I do this when messages either support or contradict something else I have heard.

_____   I can tell when my communication style may be intimidating or threatening to someone listening to me.

_____   I request and listen to feedback from others to help me improve my communication skills.

Do Something About It

Whatever your natural strengths may be when communicating and connecting with others, select actions from the following list that inspire you to challenge old behaviors and practice new ones. Consider which statements you ranked lower on pages 40–41. Improving your communication skills helps you take the lead more effectively when new situations arise.

Check the goal(s) you will set to demonstrate your leadership abilities. If you have ideas of your own that you prefer, add them on the lines provided. Then write a date by which you plan to put your goal(s) into action on the "To Do By" lines and the date you completed them on the "Did By" lines. Be sure to fill in "What I Did to Achieve My Goal(s)."

	To Do By	Did By
○ I will choose at least two of the statements on pages 40–41 that I rated as needing improvement and will practice those communication skills for at least one week.	_____	_____
○ I will observe two people who I think communicate well and record ways they give effective feedback and nonverbal messages.	_____	_____
○ I will resist getting into an argument with anyone, even if I believe my way is the right way to do something. I will listen to others' ideas rather than only think of how I want to handle the situation.	_____	_____

	To Do By	Did By
○ I will ask for feedback about my leadership potential from someone I respect. I will write down the feedback for future reference.	_____	_____

Other "Do Something About It" Ideas

○ _____	_____	_____
_____		
_____		

○ _____	_____	_____
_____		
_____		

What I Did to Achieve My Goal(s)

_____

_____

_____

_____

_____

_____

_____

_____

_____

HEAR, THERE, EVERYWHERE: ACTIVE LISTENING

SESSION • SESSION • SESSION • SESSION •

8

> Years ago, I tried to top everybody, but I don't anymore, I realized it was killing conversation. When you're always trying for a topper you aren't really listening. It ruins communication.
>
> **—Groucho Marx,** American comedian, actor, and singer

> Arthur: It's at times like this I wish I'd listened to my mother.
> Ford: Why, what did she say?
> Arthur: I don't know, I never listened.
>
> —From *The Hitchhiker's Guide to the Galaxy* by **Douglas Adams**

Being a good listener takes practice. Even if you hear someone talking, if you're not really paying attention, you may not realize what the other person is saying. Active listening requires being tuned in to what someone else says. Learning techniques to help improve active listening will go a long way in whatever leadership roles you take on.

43

Listening Blocks

What's the first thing you notice when someone talks to you? How often do you hear someone speak but then realize you're not sure what the person just said? If you are doing something other than focusing on what someone is saying (for example, silently thinking about something else), you create blocks that interfere with effective or active listening. The following "listening blocks" explain how you may appear to be listening but in fact are doing something else that prevents you from taking in what the person is saying. As you read the descriptions, think about what "listening blocks" can get in the way when you're in a leadership role.

REHEARSING

If while someone is talking you are busy silently rehearsing or planning a reply, it's harder to concentrate on what the person actually is saying.

JUDGING

If you're focused on how a person is dressed, looks, or talks, you may prejudge the person and dismiss the idea he or she is describing as unimportant or uninformed.

IDENTIFYING

If you're occupied thinking about your own experience and launch into a story before the person even finishes telling his or her story, you may lose sight of what the other person was trying to communicate.

ADVISING

If you're intent on offering just the right advice for someone's problems before the person is done talking, you might not fully understand the individual's situation.

SPARRING

If you're focused on disagreeing with what someone else is saying, you're probably not giving the other person a chance to express himself or herself.

PUT-DOWNS

If you're using sarcastic comments to put down another person's point of view, you could draw the other person into an argumentative conversation in which no one hears anything.

BEING RIGHT

If you're intent on proving your point or not admitting any wrongdoing, you may end up twisting the facts, shouting, making excuses, or even arguing the opposite of what you initially said. This may confuse and upset both you and the other person.

DERAILING

If you suddenly change the subject or joke about what is being said, you're likely to weaken a speaker's trust in you and your ability to show understanding.

SMOOTHING OVER

If you dislike conflict or want others to like you, you may appear to be supportive but not really fully engaged in the conversation.

DAY DREAMING

If you tune out while someone's talking, drifting about in your own fantasies and thoughts, you're not likely to hear a word the other person says.

For more about communication skills, see "Find Out More About It" in sessions 7 and 19.

FIND OUT MORE ABOUT IT

Now I Hear You!

When you focus on what others are saying, you can be a more effective and active listener. With active listening, you can:

- encourage a speaker to say more and reinforce your relationship with her or him.

MORE

- let a speaker know what you are hearing and if necessary ask questions when you don't understand something.

- dig deeper for information from the speaker because you are paying complete attention to the conversation and want to understand more about what's going on.

- demonstrate your respect for a speaker by acknowledging and addressing her or his feelings so emotion doesn't become an obstacle.

- guide a speaker to organize and express his or her thoughts clearly.

Think and Write About It

How actively you listen often depends on who's talking and what, if anything, the person speaking may want. But active listening in a leadership role requires a leadership attitude, no matter who's talking or what the person's asking or telling you. Complete the following sentences by describing how well you think you listen in each situation.

When someone in my family asks me to do something for her or him, I generally:

_____

_____

When a teacher or group leader presents new information, I generally:

_____

_____

When a friend invites me to do something with him or her, I generally:

_____

When someone tells me about a problem or expresses strong feelings, I generally:

_____

_____

    Now reread "Listening Blocks" on pages 44–45 and put a star next to the listening blocks that most often hinder your active listening. Referring to the listening blocks you just marked, describe which ones get in the way during the same general situations you just wrote about. Explain why you think those listening blocks prevent more active listening.

When someone in my family asks me to do something for her or him, I generally:

_____

_____

When a teacher or group leader presents new information, I generally:

_____

_____

When a friend invites me to do something with him or her, I generally:

_____

_____

When someone tells me about a problem or expresses strong feelings, I generally:

_____

_____

For these same situations, describe what you can try to do to remove the listening blocks.

When someone in my family asks me to do something for her or him, I can:

_____

_____

When a teacher or group leader presents new information, I can:

_____

_____

When a friend invites me to do something with him or her, I can:

_____

_____

When someone tells me about a problem or expresses strong feelings, I can:

_____

_____

Do Something About It

To be an active listener, it's important to focus on what others are saying and "turning off" or "tuning out" what else is going on in your head. Put your active listening skills to the test and try the following actions.

Check the goal(s) you will set to demonstrate your leadership abilities. If you have ideas of your own that you prefer, add them on the lines provided. Then write a date by which you plan to put your goal(s) into action on the "To Do By" lines and the date you completed them on the "Did By" lines. Be sure to fill in "What I Did to Achieve My Goal(s)."

	To Do By	Did By

○ I will select one of the techniques for active listening I've learned and commit to using this approach in at least five conversations. I will track how these conversations are different from others.

○ I will not watch TV, talk on my cell phone, listen to a personal music player, or play video or computer games while others are talking to me in order to genuinely pay attention to them. I will do this for at least three days.

○ I will ask for and listen to my friend's opinions when we plan to do something and not focus only on what I want to do.

○ I will listen at least three times to a positive talk radio program instead of watching a regular TV program. I will record my observations about how well the talk show host listens.

○ I will spend a day with an elder, either a grandparent or volunteering at a home for seniors, to practice my active listening skills. I will record what listening blocks sometimes get in the way of me being a good listener.

	To Do By	Did By

Other "Do Something About It" Ideas

○ _____   _____   _____

  _____

  _____

○ _____   _____   _____

  _____

  _____

What I Did to Achieve My Goal(s)

_____

_____

_____

_____

_____

_____

_____

_____

MY VALUES

SESSION • SESSION • SESSION • SESSION • SESSION

9

> *My father was very strong. . . . I don't agree with a lot of his values, but he did have a lot of integrity, and if he told us not to do something, he didn't do it either.*
>
> **—Madonna,** pop singer, dancer, actress, author

> *Open your arms to change, but don't let go of your values.*
>
> **—Dalai Lama,** 1989 Nobel Peace laureate and active member of the PeaceJam Foundation

Values make you who you are and influence what you do. Anything that's of worth to you is a value. It could be believing in a certain ideal, upholding a specific standard of behavior, or owning a certain something. Being open-minded, supporting creativity, and cherishing books are all values.

Your values naturally influence your actions as a leader, too. A test of values comes when you face decisions that require you to balance your values with those of a group. And when you act consistently with the values you express as a leader, people will likely respect you more.

51

TRY THIS

What Makes Me Who I Am

Do you know what's really important to you? Can you explain why? Each of us has our own set of values that helps determine our way of life. You probably share many similar values with the people you spend the most time with. As you get older, meet new people, and try new activities, your values are likely to change over time.

CORE VALUES are absolute values—these values tend to be unchanging, even as you grow in years and experience. Some people use the phrase *core values* interchangeably with *morals*. Morals are an individual's principles or standards with respect to right or wrong. Typically, moral standards of right and wrong come from a person's personal and cultural upbringing.

Examples of core values include: treating others as you would like to be treated, putting family first, not stealing, and telling the truth. For some people, core values are tied to specific religious or spiritual views. (Ethics, in comparison, typically are *society's* standards of right and wrong. They are tied to social norms and expectations. You'll explore ethics in session 10.)

VALUE CONFLICT occurs when you aren't sure about what you believe or want. It may also occur when you aren't clear which of your values is more critical in a situation. It's important to recognize value conflict when you are a leader because it can sway decisions you make for or on behalf of your group.

The clearer your values are to you and the more you can recognize and respect what others value, the easier it is to deal with conflict. As you complete the following statements on the lines provided, think about what's important to you and what that says about who you are.

Core values that are important to me include _____

_____

because _____

_____

The greatest influence (who or what) on the *core values* in my life includes _____

_____

because _____

_____

A value conflict I have dealt with is _____

_____

I handled it by _____

_____

A value conflict I have faced (or could face) as a leader is _____

_____

I handled (or would handle) it by _____

_____

Think and Write About It

Values are very personal in nature. In a leadership position, you may experience conflicts with your values. Sometimes being a leader requires compromising one value in order to honor another that is more important. Similarly, you may need to guide those you're leading to give and take so the group can move forward. Respond to the following questions and statements on the lines provided.

How do you determine what to do when your individual beliefs conflict with what the group you are leading needs you to do?

_____

_____

_____

Describe a situation when you felt you had to minimize your values to be accepted in a group (such as a team, a group of friends, on the street), or when you asked someone to put aside his or her values to be accepted in your group.

_____

_____

_____

Are there any situations when a leader must set aside his or her values? Explain why or why not and describe the situations.

_____

_____

_____

Do Something About It

Noticing and respecting others' values can increase your own awareness of what matters to you. Showing others what it is that is important to you demonstrates your true values.

Check the goal(s) you will set to demonstrate your leadership abilities. If you have ideas of your own that you prefer, add them on the lines provided. Then write a date by which you plan to put your goal(s) into action on the "To Do By" lines and the date you completed them on the "Did By" lines. Be sure to fill in "What I Did to Achieve My Goal(s)."

	To Do By	Did By
○ I will observe and make a list of all the places where I see values openly expressed, such as on school or rec center bulletin boards, or in television commercials, community group newsletters, or stores.	_____	_____

	To Do By	Did By
○ I will talk with someone I respect about a time when her or his values were tested or challenged by others.	_____	_____
○ I will create a personal honor code and apply it to how I behave for at least a week.	_____	_____
○ I will ask a leader in the community whose values I admire to meet others in my group and say a few words at our next meeting.	_____	_____

Other "Do Something About It" Ideas

○ _____   _____   _____

   _____

   _____

○ _____   _____   _____

   _____

   _____

What I Did to Achieve My Goal(s)

_____

_____

_____

_____

_____

DOING THE

RIGHT THING

> Our very lives depend on the ethics of strangers,
> and most of us are always strangers to other people.
>
> **—Bill Moyers,** television journalist, author

> All my growth and development led me to believe that
> if you really do the right thing . . . you're going to be
> able to do whatever you want to do with your life.
>
> **—Barbara Jordan,** first Black woman from a Southern state
> (Texas) in the U.S. House of Representatives

Choosing what is right—or most right—in a situation is making an ethical decision. You probably don't ask yourself, "Is what I'm about to do ethical?" But you may have a feeling about whether you've made a good decision. *Ethics* are society's principles of right and wrong and are tied to social expectations. (*Morals* are a person's standards of right and wrong, usually based on how you were raised. *Values* are anything that's of worth to you, such as a belief, a standard of behavior, or material possession.) If you feel uncomfortable after making a decision, your reaction may mean you didn't consider all alternatives or act ethically. Learning how to think ethically helps you gain confidence in making difficult choices and be an effective leader.

FIND OUT MORE ABOUT IT

You're Doing What?!

Facing an ethical dilemma—whether personal or as leader of a group—is never easy. As a leader, making ethical decisions calls for balancing your personal values with the needs of your group. It means respecting everyone's values and acting with integrity while still doing what's best for the group.

Knowing when a decision feels right doesn't require special powers. Everyone has internal checks and balances or a "compass" for making ethical decisions. Your ethical compass doesn't always give you an exact decision. When facing a leadership dilemma—one that requires you to make a choice between less-than-desirable alternatives—your ethical compass helps *guide* you in the best direction.

Ask yourself the following "compass" questions when you have to make a leadership or personal ethical decision:

- If a friend of mine did what I am about to do, how would I feel?

- Will I be breaking the law?

- Will this decision result in a win-win situation for everyone?

- Will I have to lie in making this decision?

- If the newspaper writes an article on what I am about to do, how will I feel?

- If my mom, dad, or other important adult in my life were watching me while making this decision, how would I feel?

- Do I have to keep my decision a secret from anyone?

- What do I feel in my gut are the possible outcomes of my decision?

- What does my conscience say?

Think and Write About It

Read the following dilemmas. Using your ethical compass, decide what you would do; sometimes your choice may feel less than ideal. Write your responses on the lines provided.

GOOD GRADES

During your first semester of high school, you become friends with Kaden, whose academic skills impress you. You ask to study together for an upcoming biology test, your worst subject. When you meet at the library, Kaden hands you a copy of the upcoming test, which he admits he took from the teacher but hasn't shared with anyone else. The biology test is the first exam of the year, and your parents expect you to get good grades. If you *don't* take the copy and you tell the teacher what Kaden has done, you may lose a new friend. It also will mean a new test for everyone—one that could be harder than the first.

What choices do you have?

_____

_____

_____

What will you do?

_____

_____

_____

AFTER THE GAME

Your mom is gone for the weekend and you're staying with your best friend. Your friend's mom, Mrs. Reese, is like a second mom to you and your mom trusts her. Mrs. Reese plans to pick up you and your friend after a basketball game at the community center Friday night. When Mrs. Reese arrives, it's obvious she's been drinking. You don't feel comfortable getting into the car. Your friend also notices the drunken behavior but tells you not to say anything when you quietly protest accepting the ride. A few other kids are waiting for rides, but you don't recognize anyone to ask for help. Even if you did see someone, you can't stay with your friend after refusing to ride with Mrs. Reese, and you're also not supposed to stay home alone all weekend. If you don't get in the car, you may lose your friendship. Mrs. Reese is urging you to get into the car and your friend starts getting in.

What choices do you have?

_____

_____

_____

What will you do?

_____

_____

_____

PARTYING

You're having a blast with friends at a party your dad has no idea you are at. The parents of the friend hosting the party are out of town. A few friends ask you to follow them into the garage to show you something. Once you get there, it's obvious several groups of kids are smoking pot. You're confused because your friends know you aren't interested in using drugs and don't respect others who do. As you turn to leave, Sam, an older kid you really admire, asks you to join the group. Assuming Sam is going to tell everyone to leave you alone, you're surprised when Sam takes a turn at smoking. Even though you don't have permission to be at the party, you know your dad will pick you up if you call him. But you also know if you call him, not only will you be in trouble, so will everyone at the party.

What choices do you have?

_____

_____

_____

What will you do?

_____

_____

_____

Do Something About It

Practicing ethical leadership can be challenging when you have to confront peer pressure and make decisions that contradict a group. This is called _ethical independence._ In contrast, thinking and acting as a group is referred to as _group think._ Although group think can be powerful and successfully produce positive results in some situations, it also can cause negative effects. Keep group think and ethical independence in mind when applying your ethical compass.

Check the goal(s) you will set to demonstrate your leadership abilities. If you have ideas of your own that you prefer, add them on the lines provided. Then write a date by which you plan to put your goal(s) into action on the "To Do By" lines and the date you completed them on the "Did By" lines. Be sure to fill in "What I Did to Achieve My Goal(s)."

	To Do By	Did By
○ I will stand up for someone who is being picked on, teased, or otherwise taken advantage of, even if it means confronting my friends.	_____	_____
○ I will read a biography or other book about a person or a group of people who confronted the unethical behavior of others. I will ask my teacher, a librarian, or another adult whose ethical behavior I admire for suggestions.	_____	_____

	To Do By	Did By

○ I will identify a conflict in my life that I need to address and use my ethical compass to make a decision.

○ I will talk with an adult I respect about an ethical decision he or she made that was a turning point in his or her life.

Other "Do Something About It" Ideas

○ _____

_____

_____

○ _____

_____

_____

What I Did to Achieve My Goal(s)

_____

_____

_____

_____

_____

_____

_____

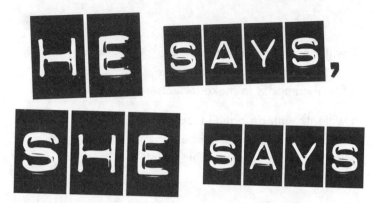

HE SAYS, SHE SAYS

> The power I exert on the courts depends on the power of my arguments, not on my gender.
>
> **—Sandra Day O'Connor,** first woman on the U.S. Supreme Court

> The hardest thing to do is to be true to yourself, especially when everybody is watching.
>
> **—Dave Chappelle,** comedian

Have you ever been judged or judged someone for being a girl or a boy? Say something to someone of the opposite sex like, "You do this because you're a girl," or "Of course you'd say that, you're a guy"? To think of a person in a certain way just because of his or her sex keeps people from really knowing and understanding each other. As a leader, the choices you make depend in part on how you view gender (the expectations people associate with each sex), as well as on others' views. But you don't need to limit your leadership style because of being male or female. Questioning and challenging gender pressures and prejudices allows you to act independently, see people as they see themselves, and keep an open mind to how others can help your team, regardless if they're female or male.

Traditional vs. Modern Leadership Styles

Gender or Sex? People often use the terms *gender* and *sex* interchangeably, but they are different.

- *Sex* describes the biological differences between male and female—that is, you are born male or female.

- *Gender* describes the norms, stereotypes, and expectations people typically associate with one sex. Based on social, cultural, religious, ethnic, and psychological values, expectations and stereotypes about gender often are influenced by your upbringing.

- *Gender identity* refers to the gender you perceive yourself to be.

To explore more about values, see session 9; for more about stereotypes, see session 12.

To say women and men have different leadership styles is a generalization. Both male and female leaders can have what are sometimes described as *masculine* traits, like taking risks, and *feminine* traits, like trusting a feeling. In the past, men generally were the only acceptable leaders. Today, people are becoming more accepting of both men and women leading—and leading in ways that reflect who they are as individuals instead of based only on gender.

Even so, gender continues to be a major factor in influencing leadership style. Understanding its effect can help clarify your actions as a leader and the decisions you make.

DID YOU KNOW?

- From 1960 to 1997, only 4 women worldwide held the primary leadership position for a country.

- Since 1997, more than two dozen additional women worldwide have held the primary leadership position for a country.*

*Worldwide Guide to Women in Leadership, www.guide2womenleaders.com (accessed August 12, 2014).

USE A STYLE THAT WORKS

To avoid relating feminine traits only to girls and women and masculine traits only to boys and men, think of feminine and masculine leadership styles as *modern* and *traditional*. Each way of leading has its own advantages and limitations.

The person leading and the situation in which the person is leading also influence leadership style. While some girls and women may naturally use more modern styles, and some boys and men may naturally use more traditional styles, these statements are generalizations.

To support more positive and productive leadership, many women and men use a leadership style that mixes modern and traditional styles.

	Traditional Leadership Style (masculine)	Modern Leadership Style (feminine)
General Approach	• Emphasizes competitiveness (plays to win) and individual responsibility • Relies on good planning and a vision to determine potential success in the future	• Emphasizes teamwork and shared responsibility • Relies on agreement and clear expectations • Follows up to make sure members meet group goals
Group Organization	• Uses hierarchy (ranks group members) • Maintains power • Expects each member to take a specific role	• Doesn't rank members • Shares power • Willing to negotiate roles
Group Organization Expectations	• Strives to win, be number one • May compromise quality to achieve better bottom line	• Strives for quality results • Less interested in comparing the group to competitors
Power	• Is controlling (uses power over others) • Objectively directs members to do their job (not influenced by anyone's emotions or prejudices)	• Is collaborative (works with others) • Shows empathy (considers others' feelings) to influence team members to act
Relationships	• Views relationships as a means to an end • Doesn't socialize with people in the group or team	• Views relationships as important in and of themselves • Is comfortable socializing with people in the group or team
Communication	• Is low key, reserved, avoids expressing emotion • Uses language and low-key manner to persuade others' support	• Is enthusiastic, energetic, willing to express emotion • Builds on open, close relationships to inspire others' support

MORE ▶

	Traditional Leadership Style (masculine)	Modern Leadership Style (feminine)
Team Participation	• Views increased participation as a breakdown of leadership influence, sometimes even a threat to group stability	• Encourages everyone to participate to support creativity and strengthen group productivity
Problem Solving	• Is rational, strategic, analytical • Is willing to take risks • Likes to review past results to determine future paths	• Is creative, seeks innovation • Is willing to trust intuition (a feeling) • Supports ideas that have no previous data
Conflict Management	• Prefers response that generally results in a win-lose situation (competition) • Also favors avoiding a conflict in hopes that it will go away	• Prefers response that results in a win-win situation • Also favors accommodating so things work for everyone
Pitching In	• Thinks helping out the team may damage image as a leader	• Usually willing to help out the team in any situation

Adapted and compiled from: Rhode, Deborah L., editor, *The Difference "Difference" Makes: Women and Leadership* (Palo Alto, CA: Stanford University Press, 2003); Evans, Gail, *Play Like a Man, Win Like a Woman* (New York: Broadway Books, 2001); Kabacoff, Robert, Ph.D., and Peters, Helen, M.A., *The Way Women and Men Lead—Different, but Equally Effective* (Portland, ME: Management Research Group, 1998), abridged results of the detailed research report "Gender Differences in Organizational Leadership: A Large Sample Study" by Robert Kabacoff, Ph.D. Norton, Dee, "Gender and Communication—Finding Common Ground," *The Leadership News: A Quarterly Newsletter on Leadership and Diversity in the Coast Guard* (Issue 7, Spring 1998, Web ed.). Schaef, Anne Wilson, *Women's Reality* (San Francisco: HarperCollins, 1992).

Think and Write About It

How you're raised, what you're expected to achieve, and who your role models are, all influence—or are influenced by—your views about gender. For each category heading from the "Traditional vs. Modern Leadership Styles" chart, identify which leadership style, modern or traditional, most *closely* matches your leadership attitudes and behavior. Remember, most people have traits from both traditional and modern leadership styles. Use the following questions to guide you as you think about your typical style. Instead of answering each question specifically, simply describe the style you choose and explain why.

GENERAL APPROACH

How would you describe your general style as a leader? Do you emphasize individual responsibilities or working together as a team? What's important for a team to succeed?

_____

_____

_____

_____

GROUP ORGANIZATION

As a leader, do you tend to assign group members specific roles or prefer to share control with everyone when getting things done?

_____

_____

_____

_____

EXPECTATIONS

How do you measure success? In competitive situations, which is more important: quality of your team's output or beating your competition?

_____

_____

_____

_____

POWER

When you're the leader, how do you get group members to do what needs to be done?

_____

_____

_____

_____

RELATIONSHIPS WITH OTHERS

How do you prefer to interact with group members when you're the leader? Do you think it's okay to become friends with group members you're leading?

_____

_____

_____

_____

COMMUNICATION

When you communicate with group members, do you show what you're really feeling and thinking? Or are you likely to express things in a more matter-of-fact manner?

_____

_____

_____

_____

TEAM PARTICIPATION

What do you consider effective team participation when you're the leader? How much is too much? When is it not enough?

PROBLEM SOLVING

Do you welcome finding new ways of solving a problem? If a group member suggests possible ideas, what do you do with his or her ideas? How comfortable are you as a leader when it comes to taking risks that may involve others?

CONFLICT MANAGEMENT

How do you prefer to tackle conflict? What role do others' opinions play when you are a leader dealing with conflict?

PITCHING IN

Do you believe it's more effective for you to lead by directing group members or working with them?

_____

_____

_____

_____

Do Something About It

By examining your attitudes about being male or female, you gain more understanding of judgments you make or support. Try choosing actions from the following goals that challenge your traditional thinking about gender and allow you to expand your mindset.

Check the goal(s) you will set to demonstrate your leadership abilities. If you have ideas of your own that you prefer, add them on the lines provided. Then write a date by which you plan to put your goal(s) into action on the "To Do By" lines and the date you completed them on the "Did By" lines. Be sure to fill in "What I Did to Achieve My Goal(s)."

	To Do By	Did By
○ I will imagine my life as if I were born the opposite sex and discuss my thoughts with someone of the opposite sex I trust.	_____	_____
○ I will pick a category from the traditional vs. modern leadership styles chart and for one week, I'll try to lead a group using the style I typically don't use.	_____	_____

	To Do By	Did By

○ I will talk with two adults I respect, one female and the other male, about their beliefs and the impact sex and gender expectations have on their life choices.

○ I will speak up if I feel someone treats me negatively based on gender and sex, or if someone makes jokes or comments that I consider critical or a put-down to either sex.

Other "Do Something About It" Ideas

○ _____

_____

_____

○ _____

_____

_____

What I Did to Achieve My Goal(s)

_____

_____

_____

_____

_____

_____

CHOOSING TOLERANCE

> *Diversity may be the hardest thing for a society to live with, and perhaps the most dangerous thing for a society to be without.*
>
> **—William Sloane Coffin Jr.,** activist and clergyman

> *When I was younger, living in an all-black neighborhood, the other kids thought I was better than them because of my light skin and straight hair. Then we moved to an all-white neighborhood and that was a culture shock.*
>
> **—Halle Berry,** actor and first Black woman to win an Academy Award

Teens talk a lot about how hard it is to feel like they fit in—and it often is. People frequently have trouble admitting their own prejudices and acknowledging when their behavior may be less than tolerant. Because a leader needs to relate to all types of people, a willingness to look inside yourself is the first step to respecting and valuing others' differences when you lead. Achieving success is easier when you create a tolerant group atmosphere. You can do that by encouraging everyone to be open-minded and to think independently so everyone feels like they matter and can make a difference.

Speaking the Same Language

Leaders who practice and expect tolerance take steps to set a positive tone with their team. When addressing sensitive racial issues, gender relations, and other concerns related to a diverse society, it helps to establish a common language. Failure to even talk about prejudices and stereotypes may negatively affect how others respect you as a leader. Following are some terms and examples to keep in mind as you talk about and confront difficult tolerance issues.

DIVERSITY

Diversity refers to including or recognizing people of different races, cultures, and backgrounds in a group or an organization.

Example: A leader who supports diversity purposely selects people different from himself or herself and one another to create a team with broad perspectives.

PREJUDICE

A prejudice is an opinion a person holds despite facts that indicate otherwise. A prejudice may also be a preconceived idea, usually unfavorable, that a person uses to make decisions or choices.

Example: A leader who demonstrates a prejudice refuses to pick a man for her team because she believes men aren't as qualified as women.

BIAS

A bias is a preference for one thing over another. A bias isn't necessarily a negative factor in a decision, except when it works against one group over another.

Example: A leader who shows a bias assigns more challenging responsibilities to older team members because he prefers using their greater experience.

STEREOTYPE

A stereotype is an assumption, exaggerated belief, or distorted truth that all individuals who have certain characteristics or are from certain backgrounds are the same. Stereotypes represent an oversimplified description of something or someone.

Example: A manager promotes a stereotype by claiming teens are lazy and late to work, and limits a high school student's hours before seeing what she or he does.

TOLERANCE

Tolerance in general means respecting the background, beliefs, and practices of other people who don't share your same background, beliefs, or practices. For leaders, tolerance involves more than "just putting up with" people's differences. It's about acknowledging and accepting who a person is and not trying to change her or him.

Example: A leader who supports tolerance promotes a team talking openly about differences and accepting those differences, without requiring members to agree with each other's views.

ISM

Ism refers to a harsh or discriminatory belief or practice, such as racism (one race is better than another), sexism (one sex is better than the other), or ageism (people of certain ages are better than others). By practicing an ism, a person favors one characteristic—usually her or his own—over another.

Example: A leader who shows racism prevents people of a different race from being on the team based on their race rather than on their abilities.

To explore sex and gender stereotypes and biases, see session 11.

FIND OUT MORE ABOUT IT

Leading with Tolerance

The degree to which you show tolerance of other people every day is a choice—*your* choice.

Even though people *believe* they treat other people as equals, they don't realize they often don't treat them equally. According to studies reviewed by Tolerance.org, many people have prejudices they're not aware of and that influence how they act toward others.

Leaders who unknowingly show their biases and prejudices can lose the respect of group members and the support they need to make things happen. People look to leaders to do the right thing, whatever the issue may be. If leaders are unaware of their biases and prejudices, they can create an environment of distrust, blame, and negativity within their team.

Many people think of biases and prejudices in terms of race, culture, religion, economic class, age, gender. But people show bias and prejudice in other ways, often toward those who are overweight, extremely shy, homeless, have a physical disability, a learning disability, or come from a home that's different from theirs.

Broadening your horizons as a leader requires recognizing and admitting any personal prejudices and stereotypes. It can be hard to step out of your comfort zone, but the more you do it, the easier it gets. Practice and promote the following principles to strengthen your tolerance skills. Tolerant leaders realize not everyone embraces diversity. But with patience and commitment, you can create an atmosphere that values the differences everyone brings to your team.

ADMIT NOT KNOWING

Be willing to learn and understand people's differences by admitting when you don't know much about their cultural backgrounds. Inviting team members to teach you shows your respect for them and increases their respect for you.

INCREASE AWARENESS

If you don't know about someone's culture or beliefs, find out more by asking questions instead of making decisions based on stereotypes or assumptions. Encourage conversations and create opportunities in which everyone can comfortably learn more about each other.

ACKNOWLEDGE AND PROMOTE DIVERSITY

Recognize that the world is increasingly diverse. Support the idea that diversity is what can make groups strong instead of pulling people apart. Regularly tell group members this is your outlook.

IMMERSE AND APPRECIATE

Find opportunities to learn about other cultures. Enjoy what's different and what's similar. Seek out new friendships, visit new places, attend cultural events and festivals, or learn a new language. When you're comfortable around people who are different from you, it shows.

MODEL TOLERANCE

Speak up when you hear slurs (insults) and let people know that saying those things is unacceptable. Make positive statements about others.

Think and Write About It

Think about past experiences as the leader or a member of a diverse group and how you may have reacted toward different members of the group. Keep those experiences as well as the session activity in mind as you write your responses to the following questions and statements.

How might showing intolerance toward others impact those looking to you for leadership?

_____

_____

_____

_____

Have you ever acted intolerantly as a leader? How did people react? Is this behavior something you want to change? Why or why not?

_____

_____

_____

_____

Think of any times when leaders have been (or are) intolerant and what they have done (or do) to justify their attitude or actions. Describe your reactions to their attitude or actions. Why do you think people sometimes accept, and in some cases support, the intolerance?

_____

_____

_____

If people of different backgrounds are in your group, what must you personally do to be an effective leader?

_____

_____

_____

_____

_____

Identify a bias or prejudice you may have toward an individual (or group of people) that is interfering with your ability to be an effective leader. Explain how you came to have this bias or prejudice and how it affects your leadership behavior.

_____

_____

_____

_____

Do Something About It

If you've ever been excluded or treated prejudicially, you know what intolerance feels like. When you can be truthful with yourself and acknowledge your biases and prejudices toward people who are different from you, you can begin to strengthen your tolerance as a leader.

Check the goal(s) you will set to demonstrate your leadership abilities. If you have ideas of your own that you prefer, add them on the lines provided. Then write a date by which you plan to put your goal(s) into action on the "To Do By" lines and the date you completed them on the "Did By" lines. Be sure to fill in "What I Did to Achieve My Goal(s)."

	To Do By	Did By
○ I will meet three new people who are different from me. I will talk openly with them to find out more about their background or culture.	_____	_____
○ I will practice leadership that demonstrates my commitment to including others by asking a few of my friends to sit with me at lunch at school with people we generally don't sit with and get to know them.	_____	_____
○ I will speak up when my friends or members of my club, team, or youth or community group make prejudicial or stereotypical comments about others.	_____	_____
○ I will invite someone of a different background to join my family for a meal or a holiday; or I will attend an event with someone from a different culture.	_____	_____

Other "Do Something About It" Ideas

○ _____   _____   _____

_____

_____

○ _____   _____   _____

_____

_____

What I Did to Achieve My Goal(s)

STRENGTH IN NUMBERS

> I am a member of a team, and I rely on the team,
> I defer to it and sacrifice for it, because the team,
> not the individual, is the ultimate champion.
>
> **—Mia Hamm,** American soccer player, youngest ever to play for U.S. National Team

> One piece of log creates a small fire, adequate to warm you up;
> add just a few more pieces to blast an immense bonfire, large
> enough to warm up your entire circle of friends; needless to
> say that individuality counts but teamwork dynamites.
>
> **—Master Jin Kwon,** South Korean martial arts master

One important goal for an effective leader is to inspire a group of people to work together as a team. When people feel like they belong to a team, achieving success often seems much more possible. By creating an atmosphere where members value each other, communicate openly, commit to the team goals, and trust one another, you can help a group shift to be a team, connecting every member to something greater than themselves as individuals.

Working as "Me" or as "We"?

Inspiring leadership is essential to help a group of people move from just getting a job done to working together as a team. When people truly feel part of a team, the sense of belonging affects attitudes and actions greatly; members believe they can accomplish things they never thought possible on their own.

If you are a member of a team rather than the leader, your leadership attitude still makes a difference in how other members feel about the team. Informal leadership in any group—team members whom others like to follow—can make or break the team as much as the formal leader. Acknowledging other team members' skills provides good opportunities to encourage them to take the lead or deal with a particular situation. Recognizing members' abilities also reinforces the belief that everyone on the team is important, whether you're the leader or not. Similarly, one of the greatest leadership roles you can take as a team member is supporting the person in charge.

Tips for Building a Team

To help motivate your group to form a team identity, it's important for you as a leader to connect with everyone involved and identify what is needed to bring everyone together. Once you figure out what's keeping individuals from connecting as a team, you can make changes that encourage them to shift from "me" to "we" thinking. To help your group be a team, keep the following tips in mind.

USE TEAM-BUILDING ACTIVITIES

Team-building activities can help group members feel more comfortable with one another. If members enjoy an activity and learn something from it to apply in real situations, they are more likely to develop interest in how they interact with one another. Encourage valuing similarities *and* differences as well. Look to work in different small groups or alternate partners to uncover unique talents.

BUILD COMMITMENT

Clearly express what you expect and why. When you communicate openly, members know what their responsibilities are and for what purpose, and everyone can share in how decisions are made and put into action. With open communication, it's easier for individual members to support goals and commit to you and everyone else.

INSTILL CONFIDENCE

An effective team leader is part of the solution, not part of the problem. Recognize what individual members bring to the team. And to help improve their skills, encourage them and respectfully provide constructive feedback. If one person is draining the team's energy and momentum, speak to that person alone. Take care not to let gossip and rumor negatively affect the team's attitude and ability to achieve success. (For more about positive feedback, see session 7.)

INSPIRE TRUST

Underlying all of these efforts is how you can inspire members of the team to trust one another and to trust you, their leader. When you act reliably (such as show up on time, do as promised, keep committed), team members know that you keep your word. They can count on you to tell the truth and on your loyalty to the team. As a result of trusting you, they are more receptive to trusting everyone else on the team. And because they feel you always have the team's best interests in mind, they are willing to make changes to achieve success together. Trust increases everyone's energy, involvement, and positive team attitude and identity.

EMPOWER OTHERS

The ancient Chinese philosopher Lao-tzu once said, "When the best leader's work is done, the people say, 'We did it ourselves!'" Enabling your team to successfully "do it themselves" shows how well you've built your team. When informal and formal leaders are all willingly on the same page, there's no need to worry about anyone sabotaging or interfering with efforts. And if you feel comfortable that individuals on your team are capable of guiding members toward the necessary goals, then you can step back and let them take the lead. To help achieve team success, members can use the same positive leadership attitudes you've upheld, whether or not you're around.

Think and Write About It

When you're part of a successful team, as a member or a leader, you feel supported and understood, you share similar interests and goals, and you often accomplish things you never thought possible on your own. As you respond to the questions and statements that follow, think about your experiences on teams as a member or a leader. Use the lines provided to write your responses.

Describe a leader who has inspired a group you've been a member of to connect as a team. If you haven't experienced such a leader, describe specific things you would like a leader to do for your group to feel more like a team.

_____

_____

_____

_____

After leading a team that has been together for a long time, you notice that members are starting to seem disconnected as a team. What do you do?

_____

_____

_____

_____

When I am leading a team, members can count on me to lead by:

_____

_____

_____

_____

In the space below, create a design for a poster to motivate an existing or imaginary team. Have fun and be creative; show what you have learned about leading a group of people and helping them to develop a positive connection as a team. Transfer your design to a larger poster board to hang where your team and others can see it.

Do Something About It

When you model a team attitude as a leader and inspire a group of people to work together successfully, others are likely to want to join your team. As a leader, selecting actions that allow you to emphasize "we" instead of "me" helps you inspire group members to become a team.

Check the goal(s) you will set to demonstrate your leadership abilities. If you have ideas of your own that you prefer, add them on the lines provided. Then write a date by which you plan to put your goal(s) into action on the "To Do By" lines and the date you completed them on the "Did By" lines. Be sure to fill in "What I Did to Achieve My Goal(s)."

	To Do By	Did By
○ I will work with a group I lead to develop a motto, saying, or slogan to help solidify our connection as a team.	_____	_____
○ I will research and lead a fun, interesting team-building activity for a group I'm part of (friends and family count!).	_____	_____

	To Do By	Did By

○ I will observe an adult I admire to see what strategies he or she uses to help a group work well together as a team.

○ I will volunteer to organize and recruit people in a class, a community group, or my family to team up and do a service project.

Other "Do Something About It" Ideas

○ _____

_____

_____

○ _____

_____

_____

What I Did to Achieve My Goal(s)

_____

_____

_____

_____

_____

_____

TURNING CONFLICT INTO COOPERATION

14

> Whenever you're in conflict with someone, there is one factor that can make the difference between damaging your relationship and deepening it. That factor is attitude.
>
> —**William James,** 19th century American philosopher and psychologist

> Conflict . . . What if we're both right?
>
> —from a poster by **Loesje,** assumed name for Dutch founder of Loesje posters

Everybody deals with conflict in his or her own way. But when disagreements arise, big or small, it means someone isn't happy with the situation. Your attitude in dealing with the issue at hand—whether you cringe at dealing with conflict or instead see it as an opportunity that may inspire something new—can make all the difference in how others regard your leadership. If you can identify the best method for helping all parties at odds to resolve their conflict, the outcome is more likely to be positive for everyone.

Managing Conflict: What's My Style?

To identify how you typically deal with conflict, respond to the following statements. Each describes a possible way for dealing with a conflict. Next to each statement, write the number that most accurately describes your behavior:

0 Not Sure   **1** Rarely   **2** Sometimes   **3** Often   **4** Always

Be sure to respond to the statements based on how you actually deal with conflict, not on how you would like to or think you should. Only use "Not Sure" if you really are not sure.

_____ A. I explore options with others to find solutions that meet everyone's needs.

_____ B. I try to negotiate and use a give-and-take approach to problem situations.

_____ C. I try to meet others' expectations.

_____ D. I argue my case and am firm about why my point of view is best.

_____ E. I gather as much information as I can and promote open communication when there is a disagreement.

_____ F. I usually say very little or try to leave as soon as possible when I find myself in an argument.

_____ G. I try to see conflicts from both sides by considering what I need, what the other people need, and what the issues are.

_____ H. I prefer to find common ground when solving problems and just move on.

_____ I. I find conflicts challenging and exciting, and enjoy the rivalry that they frequently involve.

_____ J. I am uncomfortable and anxious when I am at odds with other people.

_____ K. I try to adapt and make room for my friends' and family's preferences.

_____ L. I can figure out what needs to be done and I am usually right.

_____ M. I am willing to meet people halfway to resolve a standstill.

_____ N. I may not get what I want, but it's a small price to pay for keeping the peace.

_____ O. I steer clear of creating hard feelings by keeping disagreements with others to myself.

To figure your score, total the numbers you wrote down for each group of statements with the letters associated with the following five styles of dealing with conflict:

Accommodating: C, K, N   Avoiding: F, J, O   Collaborating: A, E, G

Competing: D, I, L   Compromising: B, H, M

For example, if you put 1, 3, and 4 for statements C, K, and N, your total for "Accommodating" would be 8. If you put 1, 1, and 1 for statements F, J, and O, your total for "Avoiding" would be 3. The style with the highest total is the approach you use most frequently; the style with the lowest total is the approach you are least likely to use. Write down your highest total and style and lowest total and style.

Highest Total and Style _____

Lowest Total and Style _____

To learn more about dealing with conflict, read the following "Managing Conflict: What Helps When?"

FIND OUT MORE ABOUT IT

Managing Conflict: What Helps When?

People may deal with conflict in all kinds of ways, but often they're unaware of how they're acting. As a leader, help manage the different ways team members react to a disagreement, whether or not they realize what they're saying or doing. Then you can better guide them to resolve the situation.

Following are five styles* people use when dealing with conflict. Each has pros and cons, depending on the situation, the personalities involved, the timeframe in which you are trying to resolve the issue, and how you tend to deal with conflict.

---

*The headings for these styles are commonly used in conflict resolution quizzes or tools. Similar terms are originally attributed to Kenneth W. Thomas, Ph.D., and Ralph H. Kilmann, Ph.D., authors of *Thomas Kilmann Conflict Mode Instrument (TKI)* (Mountain View, CA: Xicon, Inc., 2002).

COMPETING

Objective: Deal with the conflict one way, my way.
A leader who uses a competing or controlling style is aiming to achieve her or his solution.

AVOIDING

Objective: Stay quiet and remain neutral.
A leader who uses this style withdraws from conflict. The leader aims to maintain a relationship rather than to engage in a disagreement.

ACCOMMODATING

Objective: Minimize conflict or treat it as no big deal.
A leader who readily accommodates or seeks harmony when there's conflict emphasizes relationships.

COMPROMISING

Objective: Meet others in the middle.
A leader who compromises identifies which goals are worth keeping or sacrificing. Everyone's interests get considered.

COLLABORATING

Objective: Creating a win-win situation for everyone.
A leader who collaborates when there's conflict tries to resolve the issue fairly. To collaborate means to work together.

FIND OUT MORE ABOUT IT

Tips for Resolving Conflict

Whatever style you use as a leader to help a team manage a conflict, the following basic tips are helpful in any situation. Keep them in mind as you continue to take on more leadership roles.

UNDERSTAND THE CONFLICT

Consider the circumstances with an open mind. Be sure you know what all the issues are.

SEPARATE THE PEOPLE FROM THE CONFLICT

Focus on the particular issues involved, rather than on the individuals, who may feel a need to defend themselves.

BE SPECIFIC

Clearly state what needs to change rather than offer vague requests. This helps everyone involved understand what is expected.

BE FLEXIBLE

Even though you may tend to deal with conflict a certain way, try developing other styles and approaches. As new situations arise, you'll be better prepared to take the lead.

SEEK ADVICE

Even the best leaders can benefit from an outsider's perspective to manage an issue. Some people are specially trained to help resolve conflict. For example, in your school or community program, you may have peer mediators who can offer guidance. Parents or guardians, adult relatives, teachers, coaches, community leaders, or other trustworthy adults may also be able to help you resolve difficult situations objectively.

Think and Write About It

Gaining awareness of how you deal with conflict can help increase your sensitivity to other people's styles. Often, the way you respond to or help resolve team members' disagreements is influenced by previous experiences or habits. How your mom, dad, or other important adults in your life deal with conflict has a big impact as well. Keep the knowledge you gained about yourself in the session activity—as well as others' styles you've experienced—in mind while responding to the following questions and statements.

In what ways will you use your knowledge of different styles of dealing with conflict as situations arise with your friends and family?

_____

_____

_____

_____

Think about a conflict you experienced as a team member that you wish had been resolved differently. What would you have done if you had been the leader?

_____

_____

_____

_____

Think about a conflict you experienced as a leader that you wish you could have helped resolve differently. What would you have done instead?

_____

_____

_____

_____

Think about an ongoing conflict you've been struggling with as a leader. What steps can you take to achieve a meaningful outcome now?

_____

_____

_____

_____

Do Something About It

Helping a team resolve conflict productively and satisfactorily for all members takes practice. As you choose from the following goals, think about your natural style for managing conflict and what new approaches you can try.

Check the goal(s) you will set to demonstrate your leadership abilities. If you have ideas of your own that you prefer, add them on the lines provided. Then write a date by which you plan to put your goal(s) into action on the "To Do By" lines and the date you completed them on the "Did By" lines. Be sure to fill in "What I Did to Achieve My Goal(s)."

	To Do By	Did By
○ I will take my time when dealing with a team conflict to carefully consider all the issues rather than jump to conclusions about what the outcome should be.	_____	_____
○ I will watch two TV shows and observe how the characters deal with conflict. I will write about how successful the approaches were or alternative ways they could have managed the conflict better. (Alternatively, I will watch the shows with a few friends and lead a discussion about our observations.)	_____	_____
○ I will ask for feedback about my style of dealing with conflict from someone I respect. I will make notes about the feedback to keep for future reference.	_____	_____
○ I will test a different approach from my preferred style for managing conflict the next time a team conflict arises.	_____	_____

	To Do By	Did By
Other "Do Something About It" Ideas		

○ _____   _____   _____

 _____

 _____

○ _____   _____   _____

 _____

 _____

What I Did to Achieve My Goal(s)

_____

_____

_____

_____

_____

_____

_____

_____

_____

 **ALL IN FAVOR, SAY "AYE"**

> The test of courage comes when we are in the minority.
> The test of tolerance comes when we are in the majority.
>
> —**Ralph W. Sockman,** early 20th century pastor and orator for NBC radio's *National Radio Pulpit*

> The one thing that doesn't abide by majority rule is a person's conscience.
>
> —**Atticus** in *To Kill a Mockingbird* by Harper Lee

Majority rule is a common way to make a group decision. With this approach, whatever the majority decides, the entire group must follow. Each person gets a vote, but the majority—greater than 50 percent of the members of the group—wins. Majority rule offers groups a way to make decisions quickly without wasting a lot of time, particularly when the group is large. And even though everyone gets to vote, the decision doesn't necessarily serve personal interests. The minority members feel like they've lost. When groups experience close voting, for example, when 11 people agree and 10 people disagree, it may be especially challenging for leaders to keep everyone committed to the group's decision.

93

TRY THIS

The Island

If you were stranded on a remote island, what five well-known people (no family members or friends) would you choose to be with to help survive? Write your choices (the well-known people may be dead or alive) and explain why you chose these individuals. Wait to discuss your choices until everyone in your group has finished writing.

MY CHOICES

1. Name: _____

Why: _____

_____

_____

2. Name: _____

Why: _____

_____

_____

3. Name: _____

Why: _____

_____

_____

4. Name: _____

Why: _____

_____

5. Name: _____

Why: _____

_____

_____

Share your individual choices with the rest of the group.

Now as a group, identify five people everyone in the group would want to help you all survive on the island. Record the group's five choices and reasons why.

FIND OUT MORE ABOUT IT

Majority Rule: Putting It to a Vote

One of the more challenging roles a leader plays is guiding the group when making a decision. Every situation that requires a decision involves different issues, people, and goals. The reason for making the decision, whom it will affect, and how much time you have to make it are also important. To pick an option that satisfies the entire group, leaders can choose between different approaches for making the decision. One approach is *majority rule*.

WHEN TO USE MAJORITY RULE

Below are some factors in different situations and examples that point to whether using majority rule to make a decision would be most effective or appropriate.

Good Times to Use Majority Rule

- Group members have been informed of the options, which are clear-cut and not likely to be misinterpreted.

- The group has discussed an issue at length, but can't come to a common agreement.

- The group has a limited time frame to make a decision.

- Power in the group is somewhat balanced, so all members' "voices" are heard equally.

Not-So-Good Times to Use Majority Rule

- The leader realizes that if everyone doesn't agree on the same outcome, the decision will not be successful or people will try to get around it.

- Group members feel strongly about conflicting issues and believe a vote would minimize the importance of certain issues.

- The time available to make the decision is unlimited, as long as everyone agrees with the final choice.

- Power in the group is unevenly distributed and cliques in the group could easily sway a vote.

For situations like these, you would want to use another approach to decision making called *consensus rule.* You can explore consensus rule and why it would be more effective in these types of circumstances in session 16.

Think and Write About It

When a group takes time to discuss various issues before agreeing to a majority rule vote, new information or other attitudes can potentially change one member's point of view. Talking also can open the possibility for finding a better solution than one originally proposed. Eventually, though, majority rule puts the issue to a vote. This leads to a decision, even if some group members may "lose."

Describe a group experience at home, at school, with friends, at work, at camp, or somewhere else in which you *effectively* used majority rule. Explain what made this method effective in this situation?

_____

_____

_____

_____

Describe a current events issue, locally or nationally, in which majority rule was *effective*. Explain what made this method effective in this situation?

_____

_____

_____

_____

_____

Describe a group experience at home, at school, with friends, at work, at camp, or somewhere else in which majority rule was *not effective*. What made this method ineffective in this situation? How else could the decision been made?

_____

_____

_____

_____

_____

Describe a current events issue, locally or nationally, in which majority rule was *not effective*. What made this method ineffective in this situation? How else could the decision been made?

_____

_____

_____

_____

Do Something About It

To learn more about different approaches to making decisions in groups, including majority rule vote, challenge yourself to observe or participate in situations where different decision-making strategies may be in action. Consider the standard way you approach getting things done in a group, especially when you're the leader and in a position to help a group make better decisions most effectively.

Check the goal(s) you will set to demonstrate your leadership abilities. If you have ideas of your own that you prefer, add them on the lines provided. Then write a date by which you plan to put your goal(s) into action on the "To Do By" lines and the date you completed them on the "Did By" lines. Be sure to fill in "What I Did to Achieve My Goal(s)."

	To Do By	Did By
○ I will lead a discussion with my family about changing a rule at home or proposing a new one and suggest that we use majority rule vote to decide.	_____	_____
○ I will create a survey on an issue that I feel strongly about, such as recycling, and ask my friends to fill it out. Even if the majority does not support my concerns, I will see if those who do, want to help me take some action.	_____	_____
○ I will participate in the next voting process to select youth leaders in a community, school, or youth group program, or other teen club or team.	_____	_____
○ I will interview a community leader (such as a school board president, mayor, community college president, city human rights council member) regarding how he or she most effectively leads group decision-making processes. I will share what I learn with this group.	_____	_____

	To Do By	Did By

Other "Do Something About It" Ideas

○ _____   _____   _____

   _____

   _____

   _____

○ _____   _____   _____

   _____

   _____

   _____

What I Did to Achieve My Goal(s)

_____

_____

_____

_____

_____

_____

_____

_____

ALL FOR ONE AND ONE FOR ALL

> *Alone we can do so little; together we can do so much.*
>
> **—Helen Keller,** author, activist, and educator

> *A genuine leader is not a searcher for consensus,*
> *but a molder of consensus.*
>
> **—Martin Luther King Jr.,** Civil Rights leader and 1964 Nobel Peace Prize winner

Consensus rule is a group decision-making process focused on creating a win-win situation for everyone. Each person gets to voice his or her opinion, just as with majority rule. But with consensus rule, there's no voting. And a single team member who hesitates to compromise can keep the group from making a decision. This can make things complicated and time consuming. Some people feel consensus rule means giving up your individual opinion, because in order to come to a decision, you might have to compromise. But for groups that believe having everyone agree on a decision is the most important thing, consensus rule is worthwhile. To successfully lead group members to agree with one another calls for keeping discussion focused and finding a way to support everyone's interests.

FIND OUT MORE ABOUT IT

Consensus Rule: Talking It Through

When it's just you and one or two other people, it's often easy to make a group decision by flipping a coin or cutting a deck of playing cards. But when a larger number of people are concerned, those methods aren't necessarily appealing or satisfying for everybody.

Larger groups often use different approaches to make a decision more effectively, depending on the situation. One approach is *consensus rule*. You can explore another approach to group decision making called *majority rule* in session 15.

WHEN TO USE CONSENSUS RULE

The following factors in different situations point to whether using consensus rule to make a decision would be most effective or appropriate.

Good Times to Use Consensus Rule

- The leader realizes everyone must agree on the same outcome for the decision to be successful.

- Group members feel strongly about conflicting issues and believe a vote would minimize the importance of certain issues.

- The time available to make the decision is unlimited, as long as everyone agrees with the final choice.

- Power in the group is unevenly distributed and cliques in the group could easily sway a decision if determined only by having everyone vote.

Not-So-Good Times to Use Consensus Rule

- The group has a limited timeframe to make a decision.

- The group doesn't have a limited timeframe, but the time it would take the group to reach consensus could be more wisely used doing something else.

- The group can make a decision easily since there's no controversy.

- The group has been informed of the options, which are clear-cut and not likely to be misinterpreted.

- The group has discussed an issue at length but can't come to a common agreement and a vote is necessary to move the group forward.

- The group is very large and getting everyone's input wouldn't be easy or necessarily change the outcome if a vote were requested.

- The group is relatively balanced in terms of power, so the "voice" of any members in the minority won't be excluded.

Think and Write About It

Achieving consensus as a group can be challenging. It isn't unusual for groups to give up trying to reach agreement and just take a vote. Success in using consensus as a leader begins with creating an environment where everyone feels comfortable expressing his or her opinions. And when group members who often disagree can discover common interests or common ground, it is more likely everyone will support a decision.

Each of the following scenarios describes a situation in which a group needs to deal with a difficult issue. Imagine you are the group leader or well-respected team member. What steps will you take to help the group build consensus and resolve the problem?

During a youth group meeting, someone expresses that the group never does anything new and every meeting is boring. Others disagree and feel the group is doing fine.

_____

_____

_____

At the neighborhood community center where you lead tutoring activities for younger kids, one of the best-liked kids, who also tends to be a bit lazy, won't participate. Now other kids are losing interest, too.

_____

_____

During your team's last game, players were distracted and not playing their best because the captain kept making jokes when the coach gave instructions. The team lost the game and now some are angry with the coach, while others blame the captain.

Do Something About It

To learn more about consensus rule, challenge yourself to take on more decision-making roles. Think about your various circles of influence—with friends, family, a school club or youth group, an athletic team—and the role consensus can play in decision making among these groups as an alternative strategy to voting.

Check the goal(s) you will set to demonstrate your leadership abilities. If you have ideas of your own that you prefer, add them on the lines provided. Then write a date by which you plan to put your goal(s) into action on the "To Do By" lines and the date you completed them on the "Did By" lines. Be sure to fill in "What I Did to Achieve My Goal(s)."

	To Do By	Did By
○ I will plan a teen and adult meeting with others in my community youth program or school group to discuss and agree on activities, policies, or steps to take that support a teen-friendly environment.	_____	_____

	To Do By	Did By
○ When my peers complain about something they do not like or know about, I will help them find information about that issue and guide a discussion to agree on what to do.	_____	_____
○ I will run for a position on a student advisory board or student council, an athletic team, or other school or community club or organization to increase my opportunities to practice my leadership and consensus-building skills.	_____	_____

Other "Do Something About It" Ideas

○ _____   _____   _____

_____

_____

○ _____   _____   _____

_____

_____

What I Did to Achieve My Goal(s)

_____

_____

_____

_____

TAKING CHANCES

> Yes, risk taking is inherently failure-prone. Otherwise, it would be called sure-thing-taking.
>
> **—Jim McMahon,** former professional football player

> And the trouble is, if you don't risk anything, you risk even more.
>
> **—Erica Jong,** American author

One of the most challenging things for a leader to do is learning how and when to take appropriate risks. Even if you enjoy taking risks and trying new things on your own, when others are counting on you to make decisions, your willingness to lead them into the unknown may not be the same. Figuring out what risks to take and when to walk away can be a true sign of a confident leader. Sometimes the greatest successes are achieved when a leader takes action by taking risks.

Risk Taking: I Dare You To!

"I dare you to!" Ever since you were little, you've probably heard these words from friends or other kids. Maybe some grown-ups told you to ignore such challenges. In many cases, this is good advice. When you're a leader, though, taking risks may be necessary.

Taking risks means being open to the unknown—positive or negative. Speaking in front of a group or sharing a new idea with a group is a risk. These risks aren't physically dangerous, but if your speech doesn't go well, you may feel as if you're a failure; if people don't like your idea, you may lose confidence in yourself. A risk is *positive* if the outcome is likely to be successful, and *negative* if it's more likely to prevent success.

When you take positive risks, you show others your leadership attitude, as well as what you care about and your willingness to try new things. You also learn to set goals and face challenges. In the process, you'll learn more about yourself and others on your team.

For some people, trying something without knowing for certain the outcome is very unsettling. For others, the excitement of doing something new or different outweighs everything else, even if you feel like a bundle of nerves. If you're not comfortable taking risks, sticking with things as they are may be better. Yet, sometimes not taking a risk is the greater risk because you won't ever know what could have been possible.

IS THE RISK WORTH TAKING?

To help decide if a risk is right for you or your team, here are some general questions to think about:

- Would trying something new help solve a problem or is it just something that might be fun to try?

- Will taking this risk help or hurt anyone or anything?

- Will taking this risk support or break any laws or program or school policies?

- Are there small steps you can take to try out the new idea before risking too much?

- Are you willing not to take the risk if others prove or convince you that it isn't worth taking?

Be specific with yourself and your team when thinking about taking a risk. In taking a risk, you'll also want to consider a few final things, including:

- Can you identify steps to make it positive?

- Is it worth taking only at certain times or in particular situations?

- Will you uphold personal and group values without compromising ethics?

- Can you inspire the group to work together, through the ups and downs, even though you're not sure of the outcome?

- Could you fix or learn from any mistakes to become an even stronger leader?

Think and Write About It

Read the following scenarios. Imagine first that you are *ready* to take the risk described. Then imagine that you will *take* the risk described. Write your answers to the following questions on the lines provided after each scenario:

- How do you know you are ready to take this risk?

- What emotions are you feeling inside? Fear, excitement, curiosity, hope, or something else?

- What are you thinking when taking the first steps?

- When you are done, how do you feel about having taken this risk?

You have never run for a leadership position but believe you're ready to try. You want to take the steps to become a candidate at school (or youth community program or advisory board, or other group) and go through the election.

_____

_____

_____

_____

A close friend has been using drugs and drinking. You're worried because he or she has admitted to going to school and other activities under the influence. You want to confront him or her and let an adult you trust know what is going on.

_____

_____

_____

_____

Last year, a significant number of immigrant families settled in the community. A lot of long-time residents treat them disrespectfully. Teens have even started fights with new kids at the rec center because they are different. You want to attend the next city council meeting to ask that something be done to change the situation.

_____

_____

_____

_____

You've been accepted to your first choice college, which is in another state. You'll be the first one in the family, including close relatives, to attend college. Your parents want you to be closer to home. With a scholarship and a part-time job already lined up so your parents won't have to pay, you believe the decision is yours. You're going to tell them you still plan to attend your first choice.

_____

_____

_____

_____

_____

Do Something About It

   Your comfort in taking risks may be very different in a group setting than by yourself. Perhaps it's easier to try new paths when you have group members' support. Or maybe it's easier to take risks when you're the only one involved. Either way, willingness to take appropriate risks can increase your confidence and enable you to make the most of new leadership experiences.

   Check the goal(s) you will set to demonstrate your leadership abilities. If you prefer your own ideas, add them on the lines provided. Then write a date by which you plan to put your goal(s) into action on the "To Do By" lines and the date you completed them on the "Did By" lines. Be sure to fill in "What I Did to Achieve My Goal(s)."

	To Do By	Did By
○ I will sit with a new group at my community youth program or eat lunch at school with people I normally don't.	_____	_____
○ I will speak up in class or at a group meeting where I usually don't or I will try a new activity I've been curious to learn.	_____	_____
○ I will inspire my team to try something we've never done before, such as trying out for a competition or getting a new policy passed.	_____	_____
○ I will lead my team to do a project or put on an event that is completely different from anything we've done before.	_____	_____

Other "Do Something About It" Ideas   To Do By   Did By

○ _____   _____   _____
  _____
  _____

○ _____   _____   _____
  _____
  _____

What I Did to Achieve My Goal(s)

_____

_____

_____

_____

_____

_____

_____

_____

THINKING CREATIVELY

> I'd like to dedicate this to just thinking outside the box and not being afraid of who you are no matter what you do.
>
> **—Alicia Keys,** singer, songwriter, and pianist

> I dare you to think bigger, to act bigger, and to be bigger. I dare you to think creatively. I dare you to lead and inspire others... And I promise you a richer and more exciting life if you do!
>
> **—William Danforth,** physician, former Washington University chancellor, and grandson of the founder of the Ralston Purina Company

Have you ever felt stuck in a rut, frustrated, or like you wanted to think of new or different things to do? Or maybe you came up with a great idea about something, but others didn't agree. It can be discouraging, but if everyone thought alike, life would be pretty boring. Thinking creatively makes life interesting—and all kinds of things possible. Everyday situations as well as formal leadership roles provide many chances to think and act in unique ways. When you give yourself, and others you lead, the freedom to think creatively, you can achieve great success.

Be a Creative Thinker

Anyone can be a creative thinker. You don't need to be an artist or a musician. Thinking creatively means letting your mind wander to think about anything and everything. In fact, leaders who succeed over time use their imaginations in everyday circumstances, coming up with fresh ideas and encouraging others to do the same.

Lots of people depend on logic to solve problems. But being open-minded lets leaders—or anyone—discover amazing ideas that wouldn't have been tried had they stuck with tried-and-true ways.

What can you do to boost your creative thinking? To start, put aside any attitudes and actions that could get in the way of using your imagination. You can also discover untapped talent within team members simply by asking them to do something off the beaten path.

Think and Write About It

To become personally comfortable thinking creatively, it's important to fine-tune your creative thinking attitude. Read the following situations and write your ideas for how you would think creatively. Use the example to jumpstart your thinking.

EXAMPLE

The Situation

The boys' lacrosse team needs new jerseys but didn't get money this year from the youth activity fund.

Thinking Creatively About It

One of the players suggests holding a car wash or bake sale to raise the money. Another player mentions how the nursing home near his neighborhood also needs to raise some money to get a new piano. The team decides to do a fun run and use some of the money raised for the uniforms and donate the rest to the nursing home. Doing a fundraiser with a nursing home gets the team away from the standard car washes and bake sales, involves an intergenerational activity that doesn't take the players away from practice time, and also may attract a few more new fans from the nursing home.

The Situation

The first Saturday of every November, the middle school students hold Shelter Sleep Out, sleeping in the schoolyard in cardboard boxes, to raise money for a local homeless shelter. This year the weather is supposed to be bitterly cold, and you are finding it hard to motivate people to participate because of the expected weather. The shelter relies on this event to raise money for services they provide through the winter. As one of the co-leaders, what can you do to attract more participants?

Thinking Creatively About It

_____

_____

_____

The Situation

A group of regulars at the skate park, including you, want to hold an exhibition event. Getting permission requires a stamp of approval from the city council, which could take a long time. It's even possible they won't give their approval because some council members have made stereotyped comments about skateboarding teens. What ideas do you have for getting the event to take place soon and hopefully annually for the future?

Thinking Creatively About It

_____

_____

_____

The Situation

The after-school program has decided the entire inside of the building needs painting. As one of several graffiti artists who happen to participate in the program, you want to suggest that the teens in the program do the painting. How do you get the staff to agree to let you get the paint (more than just beige!) and have a go at the walls?

Thinking Creatively About It

_____

_____

_____

The Situation

Everyone says you can't be an effective leader because you messed up in middle school. But the younger kids at the rec center really look up to you, and your mentor has nominated you to be a youth coach at the center. The rec center director is hesitant, so what can you do to convince the director to pick you?

Thinking Creatively About It

_____

_____

_____

Do Something About It

Thinking creatively allows you and groups you lead to achieve more success. Strive to free up your thinking and be open to all kinds of possibilities.

Check the goal(s) you will set to demonstrate your leadership abilities. If you have ideas you prefer, add them on the lines provided. Then write a date by which you plan to put your goal(s) into action on the "To Do By" lines and the date you completed them on the "Did By" lines. Be sure to fill in "What I Did to Achieve My Goal(s)."

	To Do By	Did By
○ I will plan a fun and creative surprise activity for my group to blow off steam when working on a project or specific team goal.	_____	_____
○ I will let group members try to solve a problem using a brainstorming approach we have never tried before.	_____	_____
○ I will encourage friends, family, or people on my team who continually come up with excuses about why something won't work to instead be open to trying a new approach or idea.	_____	_____
○ I will participate in an activity I consider creative and normally wouldn't imagine myself doing.	_____	_____

Other "Do Something About It" Ideas

○ _____   _____   _____

_____

_____

○ _____   _____   _____

_____

_____

What I Did to Achieve My Goal(s)

HAVING MY VOICE HEARD

> Well, I have a microphone and you don't, so you will listen to every word I have to say!
>
> —**Robbie,** played by Adam Sandler, in the movie *The Wedding Singer*

> I didn't mean to be a role model. I just speak my truth. I guess speaking from your heart really creates a huge impact, and if I can encourage people to do that, then I would love to be a role model. If I could encourage people to use their voices loudly, then that's my reward.
>
> —**Margaret Cho,** comedian and actress

Do you get nervous speaking in front of others? That's pretty common, whether you're prepared or put on the spot. Some people are exceptional speakers in front of a small group but admit they can "lose it" in front of a large group. As a leader, it's important to fine-tune your speaking skills to keep from stumbling over your words. Getting your point across well can make all the difference between a humdrum presentation or one that keeps people on the edge of their seats. A clearly delivered message is more likely to get your voice heard and the supporters you want.

117

Getting the Point Across

Most people don't look forward to public speaking. How scary and nerve-wracking to have everyone looking at you! But speaking well can set you apart as a leader. Effective speakers get their messages heard and also build others' confidence in them.

With practice and experience, you can build confidence when trying to have your voice heard. Seize every opportunity you can—whether you're talking to the parents of kids you baby-sit, mentoring a younger student, volunteering as your youth group's spokesperson, or representing teen voices at a city council or school board meeting. Keep the following tips in mind.

GETTING READY TO SPEAK

- If you have time to prepare, then prepare!

- Organize your speech the same way you do a written paper. Include an introduction, a body, and a conclusion.

- Write notes to organize your thoughts.

SPEAKING TO AN AUDIENCE

- First take a deep breath to calm yourself.

- Remember you're talking to real people. Show the audience respect.

- Be passionate about your topic.

- Practice good grammar. Avoid mumbling and using slang or words you really don't know.

- Allow silence. Don't feel you have to fill every second with your voice.

Think and Write About It

To have your voice heard doesn't mean you have to stand in front of a large crowd or shout into a megaphone. But being prepared to express yourself well in different situations will carry your voice far. Presenting in small groups or one-to-one are terrific ways to strengthen your speaking skills for larger settings.

Read the following descriptions of different opportunities to speak up. Think about what's important to you in each situation and what you'd like to say. How can you organize and express your thoughts? Consider possible questions listeners may ask and how you can respond. Explain your detailed thoughts on the lines provided.

You're one of twelve students invited to attend a youth forum hosted by a candidate for a government office. You'd really like to ask the candidate about her interest in requiring all teens to take a driver's education class before they can get their license. Where you live, the class is optional to get your driver's license, but taking it allows you to get your license at a younger age. The candidate is proposing a fee-based class with no scholarships. Many of your friends wouldn't be able to afford the class. Describe how you'll prepare your thoughts, introduce the topic at the forum, and keep the candidate focused on the important issues.

_____

_____

_____

_____

You're co-leader for planning an upcoming annual weeklong camping trip. Because you're extremely shy, you usually let the other co-leader run group meetings. Next week, the co-leader will be out of town. You have to give an update to the three adult advisors about the camping trip and what the teens have planned and organized. Two of the adults tend to doubt the ability of your group to prepare properly and are likely to have a lot of questions. Explain how you'll get your report ready during the next week, which should include travel information, food, and a budget. Also describe ideas for what you can do if you get really nervous during the meeting.

_____

_____

_____

_____

After returning from a group counseling session, you overhear another member of the group talking loudly and laughing about something that was shared confidentially at the session. The person talking is respected by others, but also tends to bully people. When the person is finally alone, you decide you want to say something about what you overheard. Describe how you can voice your concern to this person about what he or she said and how you'll react if that person responds negatively.

It's two hours before tonight's end-of-the-season dinner banquet with players and parents. The team captain just told you that as high scorer for your team, you are expected to make a speech recognizing how well your team worked together. You've never spoken in front of such a big group before, and your team leader has asked you to be witty and entertaining. Since this isn't really your style, you'll have to plan quickly and creatively. Explain how you'll put together a meaningful speech to celebrate your team's success.

Do Something About It

Whether you're speaking to a small group of friends or a larger audience of strangers, first impressions make a big difference in capturing people's attention and getting your message heard. Make a point to practice public speaking skills when talking with family or other small groups.

Check the goal(s) you will set to demonstrate your leadership abilities. If you have ideas you prefer, add them on the lines provided. Then write a date by which you plan to put your goal(s) into action on the "To Do By" lines and the date you completed them on the "Did By" lines. Be sure to fill in "What I Did to Achieve My Goal(s)."

	To Do By	Did By
○ I will learn 10 new words to use when speaking with others.	_____	_____
○ I will volunteer as spokesperson the next time my group needs someone to talk publicly or to another organization about a particular project, event, or goal.	_____	_____
○ I will practice giving a speech in front of a mirror to improve my nonverbal communication. Then I'll practice in front of a friend or trusted adult for feedback.	_____	_____
○ I will publicly recognize the successes of my team by acknowledging them at our next organization-wide event.	_____	_____

Other "Do Something About It" Ideas

○ _____   _____   _____

_____

_____

○ _____   _____   _____

_____

_____

What I Did to Achieve My Goal(s)

MOTIVATING THE TEAM

SESSION · SESSION · SESSION · SESSION · 20

Hard work beats talent when talent doesn't work hard.

—Ceal Barry, coach, 1996 U.S. Olympic women's basketball team, and 2004 and 2005 U.S. Junior World Championship teams

People often say that motivation doesn't last. Well, neither does bathing—that's why we recommend it daily.

—Zig Ziglar, motivational speaker

Staying motivated when things don't go the way you want can be difficult. But keeping a positive attitude can help you stay committed, motivated, and inspired. Motivation is important to meet goals and finish projects. As you get to know others in your group or those you interact with every day, you'll probably discover that what motivates you may not be the same for them. To help everyone stay motivated and committed, find out what's meaningful to them and their reasons for doing things or doing them a certain way.

What Motivates You?

How often do you think about what motivates you? When you start a new project or set a personal goal? Knowing how and why you get motivated can help you understand and become more in tune with what motivates those in the group. As a leader, it's important to keep everyone wanting to work and wanting to work together until the job or task is complete.

Read the following 23 specific sources of motivation, or motivators. Next rank the items from most to least important (start with 1 being the most important). Circle your five strongest motivators and put two circles around your weakest.

_____ Getting good grades

_____ Respecting and valuing the culture and background of others

_____ Having a job that pays well

_____ Being selected for a position, such as student government, student advisory board, captain of an athletic team, camp counselor, etc.

_____ Having family approval

_____ Having friends' approval

_____ Being seen as a good person

_____ Having food

_____ Being able to do things my way

_____ Owning stuff, such as brand-name clothes and shoes, CDs, a computer, a personal music player, books, a car, etc.

_____ Achieving a goal I set for myself

_____ Partying or being social

_____ Being respected or having others look up to me or ask for my advice

_____ Being noticed or having girls or guys like me

_____ Doing the right thing

_____ Following through on responsibilities and commitments

_____ Learning new things

_____ Getting a compliment

_____ Participating in school or community activities to help others

_____ Getting the part-time job I want

_____ Having someone to look up to

_____ Believing in a cause and standing up for what I believe in

_____ Enjoying what I am doing

FIND OUT MORE ABOUT IT

Motivation: What It Takes

Some people may be very self-driven and others may need a high level of motivation to finish a task. Because people can be so different, it's important for leaders to understand various approaches to motivation.

Success Achievers and Failure Avoiders

People who tend to focus on succeeding are *success achievers*. The more success they have, the more motivated they become. For example, for an annual community holiday event, a success-achieving leader considers the occasion a success if as many people, or more, attend as the previous year. On a personal level, if you're a success achiever, getting all A's in school may be very important, because you think "nothing else is enough."

On the other hand, people who are *failure avoiders* care more about not failing than they do about succeeding. For example, on a service project, a leader who's a failure avoider is satisfied when his or her team just finishes by the deadline. Similarly, on a personal level, if you're a failure avoider, getting a low grade in a class is fine, because you may think "at least I didn't fail."

When trying to motivate people, it's human nature to assume that what motivates you to achieve is the same for them. But to effectively inspire others, whether a team or a group of friends or family, balance what motivates you with what's meaningful and motivating to those around you.

Sources of Motivation

Researchers have studied what motivates people and have identified two types of motivators: *internal* (inside a person) or *external* (outside a person). Most people aren't motivated by only one or the other, but some combination of the two. As you learn what motivates others to act, keep in mind the following internal and external motivators.

INTERNAL MOTIVATIONS

Achievement: The desire to achieve something, to work for the challenge rather than the reward, is the motivation.

Competence: The desire to master a job or do your best is the motivation.

Belief in Something: The desire to uphold personal values or morals or fight for an individual belief is the motivation.

EXTERNAL MOTIVATIONS

Power: The desire to seek control or have your opinions drive what others do is the motivation.

Affiliation: The desire to be with other people while accomplishing certain goals is the motivation.

Position: The desire to "move up the ladder" in a group to the top position is the motivation.

Heroism: The desire to do well in the eyes of someone you admire or respect, or to be like that person, is the motivation.

Motivating Others: What's a Leader to Do?

To motivate people on your team or those you interact with regularly, it helps to recognize what really matters to them. Start by showing your own enthusiasm, and providing many opportunities for everyone to be involved. The more everyone participates, the easier it is to uncover what gets each person excited. And the more excited people are, the more likely they'll stay committed and energized about the project or goals. As a result, everyone wants to see *their* team succeed. Keep these additional strategies in mind to help you motivate others:

- Help people find things that match their interests.

- Make it easy for others, especially those new to a group or situation, to speak up. Allow all perspectives and listen carefully to every idea.

- Pay attention to nonverbal communication, such as facial expressions, eye contact, and posture, as well as tone of voice. If people verbally say things that seem to differ from what they're nonverbally communicating, clarify what they mean.

- Include the individual or members of the team in setting clear goals.

- Check in to see how things have been going and what may be done differently, if necessary.

- Survey everyone privately to find out how they feel about certain situations.

Once you know what motivates a person or the team, create an atmosphere that helps them maintain excitement. People are more productive and motivated when they know:

- what they're supposed to do.

- what they can do without having to ask permission.

- how what they're doing relates to what others are doing.

- what they're doing is important and not just a token job.

- what represents a "job well done."

- what they do well.

- what they can do to improve.

- you value their efforts and membership on the team.

- you'll reward them.

- you want them to succeed in a way that *they* find meaningful.

To *keep* a positive, motivating atmosphere, remember to:

- show your own enthusiasm and excitement.

- admit when you've made a mistake.

- demonstrate that you genuinely trust others by letting them make decisions without running everything by you.

- praise people publicly, and offer any constructive criticism privately.

- show and tell others you genuinely appreciate them.

Think and Write About It

Whether you aim to achieve or just not fail, think about what drives you internally and externally to do things. Think also about your experiences with others and what you've noticed helps them stay motivated. Keep all these motivations in mind as you answer the following questions. Use the lines provided to write your responses. Reread "Motivation: What It Takes" on pages 125–128, if necessary.

Describe a time when you struggled to stay motivated. What got in the way? Were you eventually able to get motivated? Why or why not? What would have helped you stay motivated?

_____

_____

_____

Describe a time when it was very easy to stay motivated. What helped keep you motivated?

_____

_____

_____

Do you tend to be a success achiever or a failure avoider, or does it depend on the situation? In what circumstances do you tend to be one or the other? Explain.

_____

_____

_____

As a leader, you might face a group that is ready to give up. A motivational speech is the last thing they want to hear; they're tired of your enthusiasm and go-get-em attitude. What could you try to get the group newly inspired?

_____

_____

_____

Do Something About It

The more in tune you are with what motivates you and other people you lead, the easier it is to inspire a group to get or stay motivated.

Check the goal(s) you will set to demonstrate your leadership abilities. If you have ideas you prefer, add them on the lines provided. Then write a date by which you plan to put your goal(s) into action on the "To Do By" lines and the date you completed them on the "Did By" lines. Be sure to fill in "What I Did to Achieve My Goal(s)."

	To Do By	Did By
○ I will ask an adult I trust to connect me with a younger student or neighborhood teen who needs support to stay committed to his or her homework or other goals.	_____	_____

	To Do By	Did By
○ I will write a note to someone who keeps me motivated and let him or her know what this means to me.	_____	_____
○ I will stay focused on a challenging group goal or project when others give up and suggest alternative ideas to get everyone thinking positively.	_____	_____
○ I will talk with my friends about how I can help them stay motivated for personal goals they've set.	_____	_____

Other "Do Something About It" Ideas

○ _____

_____

_____

○ _____

_____

_____

What I Did to Achieve My Goal(s)

_____

_____

_____

_____

_____

SHOWING APPRECIATION, CELEBRATING SUCCESS

> It is better to lead from behind and to put others in front, especially when you celebrate victory when nice things occur. You take the front line when there is danger. Then people will appreciate your leadership.
>
> —**Nelson Mandela,** South African statesman, 1993 Nobel Prize for Peace

> Being genuinely happy for the successes of another person adds joy to our day. When one person succeeds, it demonstrates to us all that success is possible. Celebrate often!
>
> —**Rhoberta Shaler,** Canadian author and popular speaker

People want to feel appreciated. How you acknowledge or recognize others around you can make all the difference in how you relate to one another and earn their respect. When you regularly express how much you value someone, you'll find she or he is much more committed to being or working with you, no matter what the situation. A key part of succeeding as a leader is helping people feel important and celebrating their efforts and accomplishments. And by taking time to recognize contributions, you strengthen everyone's desire to be part of *your* team.

FIND OUT MORE ABOUT IT

Recognition and Rewards

When you genuinely show other people your appreciation, you let them know they matter. It can be as simple as saying "thank you," or as grand as throwing a surprise birthday party. What's important is that people are more likely to be and do their best when they know others see that they make a difference.

Strong leaders mean it when they say, "Way to go" or "We couldn't have done it without you." They pay attention to recognizing and rewarding everyone in the group. But this doesn't mean you have to acknowledge each person exactly the same way. Instead, learn what is most meaningful to each one. Then everyone can feel you sincerely value her or his contribution to the team.

Leaders who positively acknowledge and celebrate their group members' efforts create an atmosphere where people feel important. And they also are excited to keep doing more. Effective leaders realize when and how to celebrate as a team. They recognize both the small and large efforts and successes. They don't necessarily wait until the end of a project to recognize contributions or celebrate. Instead, they regularly schedule ways to honor people without overshadowing hard work still to be done. They look for personal ways to express gratitude to others for their contributions.

Try not to get too caught up in the challenges of being a strong, respected leader that you forget to mark your and others' achievements. Think creatively and get your own ideas going to make celebrating success fun.

You'll get a handout with ideas for expressing gratitude and showing others you appreciate their efforts.

Think and Write About It

As you answer the following questions, think about ways people have let you know they appreciate you, and enjoyable group celebrations that stand out for you. Write your responses on the lines provided.

How do you determine how others like to be recognized or shown appreciation?

_____

_____

_____

_____

The math team you're captain of just won the league championships. What can you do to recognize key members for their efforts and celebrate the team's success?

_____

_____

_____

_____

As the team leader for a service project, you've just learned the team's been nominated for a mayor's award for the project's success. How do you celebrate the nomination, whether or not you receive the award?

_____

_____

_____

_____

A younger kid you tutor has won an art award. You want to show how proud you are of this accomplishment. What can you do that's personally meaningful to her or him?

_____

_____

_____

_____

Do Something About It

Showing others your appreciation doesn't need to take a lot of effort, but sincerity is important. Sometimes, just saying "Way to go!" can make a world of difference. Find new ways to let people know they're important and that you couldn't succeed without them.

Check the goal(s) you will set to demonstrate your leadership abilities. If you have ideas you prefer, add them on the lines provided. Then write a date by which you plan to put your goal(s) into action on the "To Do By" lines and the date you completed them on the "Did By" lines. Be sure to fill in "What I Did to Achieve My Goal(s)."

	To Do By	Did By
○ I will invite a trusted adult who has really made a difference in my life to lunch. I will ask friends who feel the same way to join us.	_____	_____
○ I will work with my coach, mentor, teacher, or program director to make it a priority to plan a celebration for a team or committee I am on.	_____	_____
○ I will talk with my family about ways we celebrate and explore ideas about how we can recognize important milestones in our lives.	_____	_____
○ I will find out about a local community award and nominate a friend or someone I think deserves recognition.	_____	_____

Other "Do Something About It" Ideas

	To Do By	Did By
○ _____	_____	_____
_____		
_____		
_____		
○ _____	_____	_____
_____		
_____		
_____		

What I Did to Achieve My Goal(s)

_____

_____

_____

_____

_____

_____

_____

RESOURCES

Books, Magazines, and Movies

Are You Really Listening? Keys to Successful Communication by Paul J. Donoghue, Ph.D., and Mary E. Siegel, Ph.D. (Notre Dame, IN: Sorin Books, 2005)

Teaches you how to improve listening and other communication skills including paying attention and being heard.

Climb On! Dynamic Strategies for Teen Success by John R. Beede (Henderson, NV: Sierra Nevada Publishing House, 2005)

A fictional story about a teen who learns how to set goals, deal with situations, and gain insight into life by learning how to rock climb.

The Endurance: Shackleton's Legendary Antarctic Expedition, directed by George Butler (Sony Pictures, 2000)

This G-rated documentary, based on Caroline Alexander's book of the same title (New York: Knopf, 1998), presents Ernest Shackleton and his amazing story of survival in icy Antarctica.

The Good, the Bad & the Difference: How to Tell Right from Wrong in Everyday Situations by Randy Cohen (New York: Broadway Books, 2003)

A collection of ethical case studies written in "Q & A" format from the author's popular *New York Times* column.

Leadership for Student Activities

A magazine for middle and high school student leaders and their advisors working with student councils and Honor Society chapters. Issued monthly during the academic year, it covers leadership activities and topics such as diversity awareness, bullying, community service, and school decision making. *Leadership for Student Activities* is a benefit of membership in the National Association of Student Councils, the National Honor Society, and the National Junior Honor Society. Fees (currently about $65) are necessary for joining. Check with your school student council or honor society, teacher advisor, or principal to join one of the groups and receive the magazine.

My Hero: Extraordinary People on the Heroes Who Inspire Them by the My Hero Project (New York: Simon & Schuster, 2005)

A collection of essays by well-known public figures about the people who influenced their lives. A few examples include Muhammad Ali on Nelson Mandela, Dana Reeve on Christopher Reeve; Paul Newman on his father Arthur Newman, and Wynton Marsalis on Duke Ellington.

101 Ways to Reward Team Members for $20 (or Less!) by Kevin Aguanno (Ontario, Canada: Multi-Media Publications, 2004)

Inexpensive ways to recognize and motivate team members.

Rudy, directed by David Anspaugh (TriStar Pictures, 1993)

A classic, this PG-rated film is about the real-life story of underdog Rudy Ruettiger, who inspired many people with his tireless determination to play college football.

School Spirit: The Best of Leadership Magazine by the National Association for Secondary School Principals (Reston, VA: NASSP, 2002)

A collection of articles from *Leadership for Student Activities* magazine about how to improve and establish positive school spirit.

The 7 Habits of Highly Effective Teens by Sean Covey (New York: Fireside, 1998)

Provides a step-by-step guide to help you improve self-image, build friendships, resist peer pressure, achieve goals, and much more.

The Student Leadership Practices Inventory and *Student Leadership Planner: An Action Guide to Achieving Your Personal Best* by James M. Kouzes, Ph.D., and Barry Z. Posner, Ph.D. (San Francisco, CA: Jossey-Bass, 2005)

The Student Leadership Practices Inventory is a tool that emphasizes five practices to help you measure your leadership behaviors. The planner helps you improve your leadership behaviors related to the five practices.

Take Action! A Guide to Active Citizenship by Marc Kielburger and Craig Kielburger (Hoboken, NJ: John Wiley & Sons, 2002)

Covers all the basics for how you can participate in social action issues and have fun at the same time. Provides easy-to-follow guidelines for making a difference in people's lives worldwide.

Teens Can Make It Happen: Nine Steps for Success by Stedman Graham (New York: Fireside, 2000)

Bridges the gap between education and the real world to help you make plans for your goals and dreams.

Tools to Build Consensus: Facilitate Agreement in Your Group by Ron Kraybill (Harrisonburg, VA: Riverhouse ePress, 2005)

A booklet that provides clearly written, practical steps for guiding a group to consensus. Includes specific ways to deal with difficult moments and how to test for consensus.

A Whack on the Side of the Head: How You Can Be More Creative by Roger von Oech (New York: Warner Business Books, 1998)

Describes how to give your creative thinking a jumpstart and look at things from alternative viewpoints.

What Do You Really Want? How to Set a Goal and Go for It! A Guide for Teens by Beverly Bachel (Minneapolis: Free Spirit Publishing, 2016)

A step-by-step guide to goal setting to help you identify goals and put them in writing, set priorities and deadlines, overcome roadblocks, build a support system, use positive self-talk, celebrate successes, and more.

What Do You Stand For? For Teens: A Guide to Building Character by Barbara A. Lewis (Minneapolis: Free Spirit Publishing, 2005)

Ideas, activities, and resources to help you explore who you are and develop positive traits such as caring, good citizenship, empathy, respect, peacefulness, and responsibility.

Organizations and Web Sites

Big Brothers Big Sisters of America
2502 North Rocky Point Drive
Suite 550
Tampa, FL 33607
813-720-8778 • bbbs.org

Dedicated to helping kids and teens, ages 6 through 18, develop positive and lasting relationships with a mentor (a caring adult or an older teen) who can spend one-on-one time together and provide helpful, positive guidance. Some local Big Brothers Big Sisters agencies have a program called "High School Bigs," which trains and matches up high school students with younger students. Contact your local Big Brothers Big Sisters agency to see if this program is available.

DoSomething.org
1202 Lexington Avenue
Suite 305
New York, NY 10028
212-254-2390 • dosomething.org

Strives to make community service something fun and interesting for young people to do through various programs. Middle and high school students in the United States and Canada can apply to serve for a year as representatives of a Youth Advisory Council, which influences DoSomething.org programs.

Famous Speeches & Audio
history.com

Offers video and audio clips of some of the most inspirational and influential speeches of the 20th and 21st centuries.

Giraffe Heroes Project
PO Box 759
Langley, WA 98260
360-221-7989 • giraffe.org

A national nonprofit organization that honors people who stick out their necks for the common good, inspires others to do the same, and gives them the tools to succeed.

High Mountain Institute
531 County Road 5A
Leadville, CO 80461
719-486-8200 • hminet.org

Offers several outdoor adventure and leadership learning experiences for teens including "HMI Semester" (an academic and wilderness program for juniors) and "High Peaks Adventure" (a summer program for ages 14–15). Teens from diverse backgrounds have the opportunity to learn lifelong leadership skills and put them into action.

Hugh O'Brian Youth Leadership (HOBY)
PO Box 55113
Sherman Oaks, CA 91413
818-851-3980 • hoby.org

Offers leadership seminars for high school sophomores to be effective, ethical leaders at home, school, work, or in the community. Teens are selected annually from the United States, Canada, Mexico, Korea, Taiwan, Israel, and other nations.

Learning for Justice
c/o The Southern Poverty Law Center
400 Washington Avenue
Montgomery, AL 36104
334-956-8200 • learningforjustice.org

Dedicated to promoting tolerant, inclusive, hate-free environments at home and in schools and communities. Provides ideas, activities, and daily news about groups and individuals working for tolerance and fighting hate. Encourages teens to "Mix It Up" by venturing outside of usual social groups and boundaries in school and the community.

MariamMacGregor.com
817-917-4024 • mariammacgregor.com

Author Mariam G. MacGregor's Web site resource for youth leadership education and development.

MENTOR/National Mentoring Partnership
201 South Street
Suite 615
Boston, MA 02111
617-303-4600 • mentoring.org

Works with a strong network of state and local partnerships to provide mentors. To find a local mentor at their Web site, click "Mentoring Partnerships" or enter your zip code under "Connect to Mentoring Opportunities."

My Hero Project
1278 Glenneyre
Suite 286
Laguna Beach, CA 92651
949-376-5964 • myhero.com

Offers an ever-growing Internet archive of hero stories from around the world to inspire people of all ages.

National 4-H Council
7100 Connecticut Avenue
Chevy Chase, MD 20815
301-961-2800 • 4-h.org

Serves millions of young people around the United States learning leadership, citizenship, and life skills. "4-H" stands for "Head, Heart, Hands, and Health," representing the four values members work to develop through participation in 4-H programs.

PeaceJam Foundation
11200 Ralston Road
Arvada, CO 80004
303-455-2099 • peacejam.org

An international education program built around Nobel Peace Laureates who work personally with teens to share their leadership spirit, skills, and wisdom. Aims to inspire a new generation of peacemakers to change local communities and the world.

YouthBuild USA
1785 Columbus Avenue
Suite 500
Roxbury, MA 02119
617-623-9900 • youthbuild.org

An expanding network of more than 260 local programs serving rural and poor communities. Provides leadership growth opportunities for youth through academic and career programs and civic engagement to build affordable housing locally and nationally.

Youth Service America (YSA)
202-296-2992 • ysa.org

A resource center that partners with thousands of organizations to engage young people in community service and leadership activities locally, nationally, and globally. Coordinates Global Youth Service Day and promotes positive opportunities for young people to serve as decision makers in all sectors of society. An important part of this program is the YSA Global Youth Council, an advisory group of young people.